T0334638

Cambridge Elements ≡

Elements in Perception
edited by
James T. Enns
The University of British Columbia

PHYSIOLOGICAL INFLUENCES OF MUSIC IN PERCEPTION AND ACTION

Shannon E. Wright
McGill University

Valentin Bégel
McGill University

Caroline Palmer
McGill University

CAMBRIDGE
UNIVERSITY PRESS

CAMBRIDGE
UNIVERSITY PRESS

University Printing House, Cambridge CB2 8BS, United Kingdom

One Liberty Plaza, 20th Floor, New York, NY 10006, USA

477 Williamstown Road, Port Melbourne, VIC 3207, Australia

314–321, 3rd Floor, Plot 3, Splendor Forum, Jasola District Centre,
New Delhi – 110025, India

103 Penang Road, #05–06/07, Visioncrest Commercial, Singapore 238467

Cambridge University Press is part of the University of Cambridge.

It furthers the University's mission by disseminating knowledge in the pursuit of education, learning, and research at the highest international levels of excellence.

www.cambridge.org
Information on this title: www.cambridge.org/9781009044110
DOI: 10.1017/9781009043359

First published 2022

A catalogue record for this publication is available from the British Library.

ISBN 978-1-009-04411-0 Paperback
ISSN 2515-0502 (online)
ISSN 2515-0499 (print)

Additional resources for this publication at www.cambridge.org/
physiologicalinfluences

Physiological Influences of Music in Perception and Action

Elements in Perception

DOI: 10.1017/9781009043359
First published online: February 2022

Shannon E. Wright
McGill University

Valentin Bégel
McGill University

Caroline Palmer
McGill University

Author for correspondence: Caroline Palmer, caroline.palmer@mcgill.ca

Abstract: This Element reviews literature on the physiological influences of music during perception and action. It outlines how acoustic features of music influence physiological responses during passive listening, with an emphasis on comparisons of analytical approaches. It then considers specific behavioural contexts in which physiological responses to music impact perception and performance. First, it describes physiological responses to music that evoke an emotional reaction in listeners. Second, it delineates how music influences physiology during music performance and exercise. Finally, it discusses the role of music perception in pain, focusing on medical procedures and laboratory-induced pain with infants and adults.

Keywords: music perception, physiology, emotion, movement, pain

ISBNs: 9781009044110 (PB), 9781009043359 (OC)
ISSNs: 2515-0502 (online), 2515-0499 (print)

Contents

1 Introduction

Music has long been used as an instrument of pleasure and soothing, from lullabies during infancy to nostalgic music of previous eras in later adulthood. Only recently have scientists pursued the physiological changes wrought by music that enable it to serve as a non-pharmacologic analgesic, mood enhancer, and driver of rhythmic actions such as dance, rowing, and synchronised sports. The rhythmic properties of music offer a popular arousing training regimen for running, dancing, weightlifting, and a wide array of human activities that require endurance. Furthermore, the pleasurable outcomes of music have been implemented as a non-medicinal intervention in healthcare settings. It is important, therefore, to understand which physiological mechanisms are influenced by music and over what time course.

This Element focuses on the physiological influences of music on perception and action. We review experimental studies that manipulated the presence or type of music and measured physiological changes in relation to behavioural changes in perception or action. Common physiological measures include cardiac rhythms, blood pressure, pulse, electrodermal activity (EDA, also referred to as galvanic skin response [GSR]), and breathing rate. Some studies include additional measures such as blood lactate, salivary cortisol, and pupil dilation. As several reviews of the effects of music on a wide range of behaviours have been published in the last decade or more (cf. Eerola & Vuoskoski, 2013; Hartling et al., 2009; Karageorghis et al., 2011; Nilsson, 2008), we focus here on studies published since 2010. Table 1 summarises the studies reviewed in this Element, classified by both the acoustic variables that were manipulated in the music and the physiological variables measured (a single paper may appear in more than one row or column). Peer-reviewed articles that met both inclusion criteria shown in Table 1 of manipulating acoustic variables and measuring physiological variables were retrieved from PubMed, PsycINFO, and Google Scholar. Thus, the collection of articles is selective (rather than exhaustive). Each cell in Table 1 contains hyperlinks to the set of readings, to aid readers who wish to pursue specific studies.

The sections of this Element are ordered from a focus on general influences of music on physiology during perception and action to more specific behavioural contexts. First, we review general physiological influences of music during perception, with an eye to specific musical features and individual differences. We then review three primary areas in which physiological influences of music have been addressed in perception and action. The three primary areas are emotional response to music, physiological influences of music during movement, and pain response to music. Finally, we end with a discussion of current

Table 1 Categorisation of studies by physiological measures and acoustic variables

	Acoustic Variables		
Physiological measures	Tempo	Intensity	Other variables
Heart rate (electrode leads)	Coutinho & Cangelosi (2011); Krabs et al. (2015); Labbé et al. (2020); Mütze et al. (2018); Nomura et al. (2013); Ooishi et al. (2017); Watanabe et al. (2015, 2017)	Cheng & Tsai (2016); Mikutta et al. (2013)	Dellacherie et al. (2011); Lima et al. (2017); Lynar et al. (2017); Shabani et al. (2016); Tang et al. (2018); Tekgündüz et al. (2019); Vieillard et al. (2012); White & Rickard (2016)
Heart rate (chest and watch straps)	Almeida et al. (2015); Bacon et al. (2012); Egermann et al. (2015); Eliakim et al. (2012); Hutchinson & O'Neil (2020); Jones et al. (2017); Karageorghis et al. (2018); Lee & Kimmerly (2016); Waterhouse et al. (2010)		Cutrufello et al. (2020); Di Cagno et al. (2016); Lee et al. (2017); Rasteiro et al. (2020); Stork et al. (2019); Tsai & Chen (2015)
Heart rate (other measurements)	Chuen et al. (2016); Desai et al. (2015); Dyer & McKune (2013); Lim et al. (2014); Patania et al. (2020); Sills & Todd (2015); Tan et al. (2014); van Dyck et al. (2017)	Chuen et al. (2016)	Amini et al. (2013); Bood et al. (2013); Bullack et al. (2018); Cavaiuolo et al. (2015); Egermann et al. (2013); Eliakim et al. (2013); Juslin et al. (2014); Rossi et al. (2018); Savitha et al. (2013)
Time-domain HRV	Almeida et al. (2015); Bretherton et al. (2019); da Silva et al. (2014a, 2014b); Egermann et al. (2015); Krabs et al. (2015); van der Zwaag et al. (2011)	do Amaral et al. (2015)	Santana et al. (2017)

Table 1 (cont.)

	Acoustic Variables		
Physiological measures	Tempo	Intensity	Other variables
Frequency-domain HRV	Bretherton et al. (2019); da Silva et al. (2014a, 2014b); Egermann et al. (2015); Krabs et al. (2015); Ooishi et al. (2017); Watanabe et al. (2015)		Lynar et al. (2017); Santana et al. (2017)
Blood pressure	Desai et al. (2015); Karageorghis et al. (2018); Savitha et al. (2010)		Garcia & Hand (2016); Harmat et al. (2011); Labrague & McEnroe-Petitte (2016); Lee et al. (2017)
Pulse rate	Desai et al. (2015); Savitha et al. (2010)		Garcia & Hand (2016); Labrague & McEnroe-Petitte (2016)
Skin conductance (tonic/other measures)	Egermann et al. (2015); Krabs et al. (2015); van der Zwaag et al. (2011)		Bullack et al. (2018); Juslin et al. (2014, 2015); Lynar et al. (2017); Vieillard et al. (2012); White & Rickard (2016)
Skin conductance (phasic measures)	Chuen et al. (2016); Egermann et al. (2015)	Bradshaw et al. (2011); Chuen et al. (2016); Olsen & Stevens (2013)	Bannister (2020); Bannister & Eerola (2018); Dellacherie et al. (2011); Egermann et al. (2013); Solberg & Dibben (2019); Tsai & Chen (2015)
Respiration rate	Chuen et al. (2016); Egermann et al. (2015); Jones et al. (2017); Labbé et al. (2020); Mollakazemi et al. (2019); Mütze et al. (2018); Nassrallah et al. (2013)	Cheng & Tsai (2016); Chuen et al. (2016)	Bernardi et al. (2017a, 2017b); Bullack et al. (2018); Egermann et al. (2013); Harmat et al. (2011); Lee et al. (2017); Lynar et al. (2017); Müller & Lindenberger (2011)

Table 1 (cont.)

Physiological measures	Acoustic Variables		
	Tempo	Intensity	Other variables
Respiration depth			Tsai & Chen (2015); Vickhoff et al. (2013)
Oxygen consumption /saturation	Almeida et al. (2015); Bacon et al. (2012); Dyer & McKune (2013); Hoffmann & Bardy (2015); Hoffmann et al. (2012); Jones et al. (2017); Lim et al. (2014)		Amini et al. (2013); Cavaiuolo et al. (2015); Fritz et al. (2013); Lima et al. (2017); Rossi et al. (2018); Savitha et al. (2013); Tang et al. (2018); Tekgündüz et al. (2019)
Blood lactate	Eliakim et al. (2012); Hutchinson & O'Neil (2020); Jones et al. (2017); Lee & Kimmerly (2016)		Eliakim et al. (2013); Rasteiro et al. (2020); Terry et al. (2012)

Note Studies reviewed in this Element, published since 2010 in peer-reviewed journals that reported physiological variables and experimental manipulation of music. Studies are organised by physiological measures reported and acoustic variables manipulated; hyperlinks to full references are included. Each study was categorised first by tempo and intensity acoustic variables; the 'Other variables' column contains remaining (non-overlapping) entries. Studies that contain multiple physiological measures appear in multiple rows.

trends, including clinical applications of music, and promising future directions in the study of how music influences human physiology during perception and action.

2 Basic Physiological Response to Music

It is important to consider how musical sound affects basic responses of our physiological system before we address higher-level responses to music such as emotional response. The autonomic nervous system (ANS) plays a key role in modulating arousal needed for movement ability, and ANS-regulated processes such as heart rate, respiration, or skin conductance can serve as physiological markers of stress, arousal, or emotional state (Shaffer et al., 2014). Understanding the basic effects of musical sound on the ANS is thus of great importance to the relationships among musical sound, physiological response, and psychological states (for reviews, see Cervellin & Lippi, 2011; Koelsch & Jancke, 2015; Trappe, 2010; Valenti et al., 2012; Zekveld et al., 2018). This section presents a) an overview of different physiological measures and their response to tempo, the rate of a musical sequence often expressed in number of beats per minute (BPM), and b) intensity dimensions of musical sound, with particular emphasis on cardiac activity during music perception.

2.1 Definitions of Physiological Measures

Electrodermal activity (EDA) refers to the electrical conductivity on the surface of one's skin, and it is commonly measured by attaching small electrodes to the fingers or palmar surface of the hand. Slow-changing or tonic electrical conductivity is known as skin conductance level (SCL), and fast-changing or phasic change in skin conductivity is known as skin conductance response (SCR; Critchley & Nagai, 2013). The slow-changing tonic component adjusts over the course of an experimental session, and the fast-changing phasic component is linked to stimulus presentation. EDA is a physiological marker of sympathetic nervous system (SNS) activity (Critchley & Nagai, 2013); increases in skin conductance generally indicate an increase in physiological arousal. Researchers are often interested in the size of the SCR as well as the time course of the SCR during stimulus presentation.

Respiration, another common physiological marker, is often measured as respiration rate (inhalations or exhalations per minute) or respiration depth (breath volume). A greater number of respiration cycles per minute typically reflects increased physiological arousal and is common during physical exertion. Respiration rate is easy to measure in a non-invasive manner as it can be measured with a respiration belt that is worn around the chest or torso. Respiratory depth can also be measured non-invasively with a mask to collect gas exchange and ventilation (Hoffmann et al., 2012).

Cardiac activity is commonly measured by both heart rate and heart rate variability (HRV). As with respiration, cardiac activity is easily measured in a non-invasive manner. The gold standard for measuring cardiac activity is electrocardiography (ECG), which involves attaching electrodes to the chest. However, consumer-level chest straps with built-in electrodes are a reliable and frequently used alternative to ECG in research settings. Heart rate can be quantified as the average number of heartbeats per minute or by the average inter-heartbeat interval between two successive beats (referred to as RR interval). Larger RR intervals indicate a slower heartbeat, while smaller RR intervals indicate a faster heartbeat. The time between heartbeats is normally variable;

this variability is known as heart rate variability (HRV), and it can be attenuated or enhanced by different physiological inputs to the heart as well as by demands placed on an organism.

A large source of resting-state HRV is respiratory sinus arrhythmia (RSA), the speeding up of heartbeats as one breathes in and the slowing down of heartbeats as one breathes out. One primary mechanism of the RSA is the vagus nerve, which is the major parasympathetic nervous system (PNS) input to the heart. The PNS is the branch of the autonomic nervous system that is involved in lowering physiological arousal (the 'rest and digest' branch). This means that heart rate is typically slowed down when there is greater PNS input to the heart. During inhalation, vagus nerve input to the heart is typically attenuated which leads to increases in heart rate. Then, during exhalation, vagus nerve input to the heart increases, and heart rate decreases. This creates resting-state variability in the heartbeat period that is linked to respiration. At rest (low arousal), HRV is typically high. External demands on an organism such as movement or cognitive effort that require an increased state of physiological arousal or alertness typically result in an increase in HR and a decrease in HRV. Common time-domain measures of HRV include the standard deviation of normal-to-normal heartbeats (SDNN) and the root mean square of successive differences in heartbeats (RMSSD). The SDNN captures overall HRV, while the RMSSD captures short-term variability.

It is important to note that HRV is measured at different timescales, and oscillations at these timescales reflect the influence of different inputs on the heart. The timescales of cardiac oscillations are commonly quantified as being ultra-low frequency (<0.0033 Hz), very low frequency (0.0033–0.04 Hz), low frequency (0.04–0.15 Hz), and high frequency (0.15–0.40 Hz). Of primary interest in research on the influence of music on HRV is the power present at the low- and high-frequency ranges. High-frequency oscillations in heartbeats are largely attributed to respiration (RSA) and PNS modulation of the heart (Shaffer et al., 2014). Low-frequency oscillations may be a combination of blood pressure changes, SNS activity (the 'fight or flight' or stimulating branch of the ANS), and PNS activity when breathing rates are slow (Porges, 2007; Shaffer et al., 2014). Researchers frequently decompose cardiac signal measurements into frequency components to identify the potential physiological source of HRV and subsequently whether a task or a stimulus has altered PNS and SNS activity. A commonly used frequency-domain metric to quantify sympathetic–parasympathetic activity is the low-frequency to high-frequency power ratio. However, as low-frequency cardiac oscillations may be a result of multiple physiological inputs acting on the heart, the physiological interpretation of the low- to high-frequency power ratio is not quite so straightforward

(Berntson et al., 1997; Task Force of the European Society of Cardiology and the North American Society of Pacing and Electrophysiology, 1996).

Other physiological measures that are covered in this section are pupil dilation and blood lactate concentration. Pupil dilation refers to the constriction of one's pupils in response to a stimulus. The pupil is of course highly sensitive to environmental light levels, but research suggests that pupil dilation also occurs in response to tasks of varying cognitive load and that pupil size may be a physiological marker of arousal (Zekveld et al., 2018) as it is influenced by both the PNS (constriction) and the SNS (dilation). Blood lactate concentration is used as a physiological marker of physical exercise performance often in endurance-testing paradigms (Jacobs, 1986). Typically, as one exercises for longer periods, exercises more strenuously over time, or enters a recovery period following intense physical exercise, blood lactate begins to accumulate and can interfere with optimal muscle functioning (Goodwin et al., 2007; Jacobs, 1986). As shown in Table 1, tempo and intensity were the most often manipulated musical parameters. The studies listed under 'other variables' manipulated a range of musical variables including musical genre, pitch, timbre, rhythmic complexity, musical mode, and metre. Table 1 also shows that physiological measurements tended to fall in the following categories: cardiac activity (heart rate, HRV, pulse, and blood pressure), SCR, and oxygenation (respiration rate and depth, oxygen consumption, and blood lactate levels).

2.2 Musical Tempo Affects Autonomic Activity

Imagine that you are asked to generate a hypothesis about how a fast-tempo piece of music and a slow-tempo piece of music will influence your arousal level. A reasonable hypothesis might be: a fast musical tempo will lead to increased physiological arousal, such that a listener experiences a faster heart rate and breathing rate compared to when they listen to a slow musical tempo (or no music at all). The expectation in this hypothesis is that a faster musical tempo increases physiological activity via increased arousal, and a slower musical tempo decreases physiological activity and arousal. Indeed, a version of this hypothesis appears in many studies that ask participants to listen to musical excerpts of different tempi while measuring heart rate, HRV, respiration, and SCR. Readers should click here (Audio 1–5) to hear an example of the same piece of music, 'Baa Baa Black Sheep', sounded at a range of tempi similar to the range used in the reviewed studies (files also available at www.cambridge.org/physiologicalinfluences).

Investigations of the effect of musical tempo on rhythmic ANS activity, such as heart rate or respiration, are ultimately grounded in biological notions of rhythmic entrainment: when two or more oscillators become coupled or

Audio 1 Baa Baa Black Sheep at Slow Tempo (60 BMP)

Audio 2 Baa Baa Black Sheep at Moderate Tempo (90 BMP)

Audio 3 Baa Baa Black Sheep at Lively Tempo (120 BMP)

Audio 4 Baa Baa Black Sheep at Fast Tempo (150 BMP)

Audio 5 Baa Baa Black Sheep at Faster Tempo (180 BMP)

matched in period (inverse of frequency). Entrainment is distinct from synchronisation of two systems: two events may occur simultaneously in time (in synchrony), but neither system's endogenous behaviour is persistently altered (Bittman, 2021). In the case of music and the heart, the music tempo is the periodic stimulus to which heartbeats might alter their frequency. The next section reviews studies that tested how musical sound impacts physiological activity. Some studies evaluate the theoretical framework of entrainment by examining the relationship between changes in tempo and heart rate. One reason that some studies tend to include only fast-tempo or only slow-tempo music may be to avoid carryover effects in ANS activation among conditions within a single experimental session. The final section reviews studies that compare musical intensity with ANS activation during music listening.

2.2.1 Fast Tempo and Increased Physiological Arousal

A fast musical tempo has generally been shown to have a stimulating effect on listeners' ANS activity; this finding holds not only for listening to musical excerpts but also for sequences of tones (pitches) that have rhythm but no melody. In a pilot study, Nomura et al. (2013) compared listeners' heart rates in three conditions: hearing music (instrumental jazz) at its original tempo (approximately 3:1 ratio of musical beats to heartbeats), 10 per cent faster tempo music, and 10 per cent slower tempo music. The listeners' mean HR was faster during the fast tempo compared to the slow-tempo music. Da Silva et al. (2014a, 2014b) compared listeners' cardiac activity (HRV) during a fast-tempo music piece (heavy metal, tempo not provided), a slow music piece (Baroque music, tempo not provided), and a silent baseline. Da Silva et al.'s 2014a study reported no differences between conditions in HRV (SDNN, RMSSD, high-frequency HRV, and low-frequency HRV). In contrast, da Silva et al. (2014b) found that both music conditions decreased listeners' low-frequency HRV from baseline and that overall HRV (SDNN) and high-frequency HRV decreased from baseline to the fast-tempo music condition, possibly indicating a reduction in PNS activity. Both studies used the same music excerpts, but da Silva et al. (2014a) used twenty-minute musical excerpts, while da Silva et al. (2014b) used five-minute musical excerpts. Discrepancies in their results may thus have been influenced by the length of exposure to a musical excerpt, suggesting that cardiac responses to musical tempo vary with musical duration.

Sills and Todd (2015) compared listeners' mean HR during music listening (excerpts of various genres and tempi, tempi not reported) and silent baseline. Faster tempo musical excerpts did not result in listeners' increased HR relative to slower tempo musical excerpts or silent baseline. It should be noted, however, that da Silva et al. (2014a, 2014b) and Sills and Todd (2015) used musical pieces of varying genres, which may have confounded the role of tempo on ANS activity and prevented a clear conclusion as to whether musical tempo entrained heart rates.

Musical tempo is dynamic in time, meaning that tempo fluctuations occur during a musical piece and may have important effects on ANS activity. Chuen et al. (2016) played sequences of 24–28 isochronous tones to listeners. Cardiac activity (HR), SCR, and respiration rate were measured during stable tone sequences (750 ms inter-tone interval [ITI]), tone sequences with an increase in tempo mid-sequence (600 ms ITI, 500 ms ITI, or 429 ms ITI), and silent baseline. In the stable condition, HR tended to decrease over time relative to baseline. In the tempo change conditions, HR increased for the 600 ms and 500 ms ITI alterations relative to the stable condition. Larger magnitude SCR measures were observed at the largest tempo increase (429 ms ITI) indicating a proportional change in SCR to stimulus tempo change. There was no effect on respiration rate. To explain these findings, Chuen et al. (2016) discuss the orienting response, holding that changes in acoustic parameters such as tempo may trigger an ANS response, reflected in cardiac, respiratory, and skin conductance measures, due to their novelty. More fine-grained analyses of ANS activity during music listening are needed to fully evaluate the role of the orienting response on ANS changes during music listening and understand how cardiac, respiratory, and skin conductance activity is modulated during music listening.

Additional evidence that a fast musical tempo has a stimulating effect on the ANS comes from studies that investigated the role of breathing rate in cardiac changes to fast-tempo music (Watanabe et al., 2015). In all experiments, listeners were instructed to fix their breathing rates, guided by a silent visual metronome. In one experiment, Watanabe et al. (2015) manipulated tone sequence tempo (slow = 60 BPM and fast = 80 BPM) and breathing rate (slow = 15 breaths per minute and fast = 20 breaths per minute). They compared cardiac activity (HR and HRV) during tone sequence listening and silent baseline (respiration rate fixed at 15 breaths per minute). Heart rate increased when listeners breathed at the fast breathing rate and heard the fast-tempo (80 BPM) tone sequences, compared with all other conditions. High-frequency HRV was lower during the fast breathing, fast-tempo condition compared to silent baseline. In another experiment, Watanabe et al. (2015) fixed listeners' breathing rates to 20 breaths per minute during tone sequence listening and silent baseline (Watanabe et al., 2015). Heart rate was again faster when listeners heard the fast-tempo (80 BPM) tone sequence compared to the slow-tempo (60 BPM) and baseline conditions. However, high-frequency HRV did not differ between any conditions (Watanabe et al., 2015), suggesting slower baseline respiration rates in the first experiment may have contributed to the HRV findings.

To test whether synchronisation between listeners' breathing and the musical tempo had accounted for changes in cardiac activity in the earlier experiment, Watanabe et al. (2015) compared cardiac activity (HR and HRV) during a different range of musical tempo conditions (78 BPM, 80 BPM, and 82 BPM) and silent baseline (respiration rate fixed at 15 breaths per minute). Mean heart rate increased during all musical tempo conditions relative to baseline, but there were no changes in HRV. Together, Watanabe et al.'s (2015) findings show that breathing rates may influence HR and HRV during listening to fast-tempo music, but changes in mean HR with fast breathing and fast-tempo music were not explained by synchronisation of the listeners' respiration with the musical tempo.

There is also contradictory evidence to the interpretation that breathing rate directly influences ANS activity changes during listening to simple tone sequences. Mollakazemi et al. (2019) compared listeners' cardiac activity (HR) and respiration rate during unfamiliar fast-tempo music, unfamiliar slow-tempo music, a self-selected song (uncontrolled tempo), and a silent baseline. They found increases in respiration during the fast tempo, slow tempo, and self-selected song conditions but no change in HR across any conditions. In another study, Mütze et al. (2018) manipulated in real time the tempo of a simple Djembé beat to create four music listening conditions: tempo matched to the listener's baseline HR, tempo 25 per cent faster, tempo 40 per cent faster, and tempo 55 per cent faster than the listener's HR. Listeners' HR and respiration rate were measured during the music conditions and were compared with a silent baseline condition. Respiration rates increased when the music tempo was 40 per cent faster than the listeners' HR, but HR did not increase during perception of any of the tempo manipulations. Importantly, this study by Mütze et al. (2018) is one of the few studies to explicitly examine period entrainment and phase alignment of heartbeats with the musical beats. They found no group-level evidence of cardiac period entrainment or phase alignment to music; rather, the researchers observed large inter-individual differences in the stability of the cardiac period as well as the phase relationship between heartbeats and musical beats.

Manipulations of stimulus tempo as a function of individuals' baseline heart rates are particularly important because the effect of music tempo on HR has been shown to depend upon an individual's resting HR. Watanabe et al. (2017) showed that while listening to a tone sequence at 80 BPM, individuals with a slow resting HR (60–70 BPM) had an increase in HR while individuals with a fast resting HR (80+ BPM) had no change or a decrease in HR. Mütze et al.'s (2018) study titrated the tempo manipulations relative to individual differences in baseline HR as well as real-time changes in HR, but no group-level change in cardiac activity was observed. One primary difference between Mütze et al. (2018) and Watanabe et al. (2017) is the control of breathing rates. Mütze et al. (2018) did not control listeners' respiration rates whereas Watanabe et al. (2017) instructed listeners to breathe at a rate of 20 breaths per minute. As cardiac activity is directly influenced by respiratory activity, the experimental manipulations of breathing may have accounted for their contrasting findings.

Whether listeners' natural breathing alterations during music listening modulate their cardiac activity is an open question. Given that some studies showed no increased cardiac or respiratory responses to fast music tempi, the evidence for a relationship between fast tempo and a stimulatory effect on ANS activity (increased heart rate and respiration, decreased HRV) is still preliminary. One methodological consideration for future studies is how to define the range of musical tempo to which a listener may be sensitive. Individual differences in baseline HR, breathing rates, and preferences for musical tempi, suggest that a one-size-fits-all fast-tempo manipulation may not be the best approach to determine the effects of fast-tempo music on respiratory and cardiac activity. In addition, studies that report the musical tempo consider different values for a 'fast' range (e.g., 80 BPM in Watanabe et al., 2017 compared to 120 BPM in Chuen et al., 2016). These issues further obscure an answer to the question, 'How fast is fast?' and whether rhythmic physiological activity is influenced or entrained by musical tempo. The next section reviews the relationship between respiratory and cardiac responses to slow-tempo music.

2.2.2 Slow Tempo and Decreased Physiological Arousal

Shifts toward a more relaxed or low-arousal physiological state (decreased HR, increased HRV, decreased respiration rate, and decreased SCR) that are caused by slow-tempo music have been observed only in some studies. Ooishi et al. (2017) presented music by Chopin and compared listeners' heart rates as they heard slow-tempo excerpts (56 BPM), extremely fast-tempo excerpts (233 BPM), or a silent baseline. Although there was no effect of fast-tempo music on listeners' heart rate, slow-tempo music (56 BPM) led to slower heart rate and increased high-frequency HRV compared to the silent baseline. This represents a potential shift toward PNS dominance (decreased physiological arousal) with slow-tempo music. Van Dyck et al. (2017) used ambient instrumental music and compared listeners' heart rates when they listened to music with a tempo matching their individual baseline heart rate (generally between

60 and 85 BPM), a tempo faster or slower (±15%, ±30%, and ±45%) than their individual baseline heart rate, and a silent baseline. Similar to Ooishi et al. (2017), Van Dyck et al. observed slower heart rates while individuals listened to slow pieces of music (–30% and –45%) relative to when they listened to fast pieces of music but not relative to silent baseline (Ooishi's slow-tempo condition differed only from the silent baseline). Also, similar to Ooishi, Van Dyck found no effect of fast-tempo music on cardiac activity. Thus, these results support a relaxing effect of slow-tempo music on the ANS when the tempo differences are extreme or when the tempo is titrated to listeners' baseline heart rates.

Effects of musical tempo on physiological measures have also been examined in tempo manipulations of the same music presented across trials. Bretherton et al. (2019) presented a familiar musical tune ('Baa Baa Black Sheep'; readers can listen to the sound examples found here at www.cambridge .org/physiologicalinfluences) in a condition with tempo-increasing order across trials (60 BPM to 180 BPM, increasing by 30 BPM), a condition with tempo-decreasing order across trials (180 BPM to 60 BPM, decreasing by 30 BPM), and a constant tempo condition (120 BPM); a fourth condition of a silent baseline was included. Respiration and HRV were compared between conditions as well as within tempo-increasing and tempo-decreasing conditions. Results showed that high-frequency HRV was greatest for the slowest tempi in the decreasing tempo sequences, but overall, HRV was lower in tempo-decreasing versus tempo-increasing sequences (Bretherton et al., 2019). These findings suggest that slow music tempi and changes in musical tempo may not have a consistent relaxing effect on the ANS.

In sum, definitions of fast- and slow-tempo music have not been standardised across studies; sometimes, the experimental manipulations may not be sufficiently large to gauge the physiological effects of a musical tempo. In addition, manipulations of tempo within a musical piece are largely absent from the majority of studies that investigate how music tempo influences physiological response. Tracking continuous changes in both physiology and acoustic signals during music listening while manipulating tempo may help address discrepancies in the current findings. This approach would also inform on potential entrainment effects of musical tempo on the ANS, as changes in ANS activity could be monitored across a piece of music.

Overall, these studies support only a weakly coupled relationship between mean heart rate and musical tempo. There has not been much consideration of listeners' breathing patterns during music listening, despite the fact that they are closely coupled with cardiac activity. This may be due in part to the dominance in the literature of linear measures (such as mean rate and variability) of physiological activity during music listening. Linear measures assume stationarity of the signals being analysed; however, it is well-documented that both musical tempo and physiological signals (cardiac and respiratory measures) are not stationary and exhibit periodic change. As linear measures fail to capture the non-linear dynamics of physiological responses, important patterns or changes in physiological signals in response to music may go undetected. We are currently investigating physiological responses to music perception and performance with non-linear analysis methods, which will be described in upcoming sections.

2.3 Musical Intensity Affects ANS Activity

Several findings suggest that an increased intensity (loudness) of a musical piece or a rhythmic tone sequence elicit an increase in physiological arousal. Listeners who heard heavy metal music and classical Baroque music in various loudness ranges (60–70 dB, 70–80 dB, and 80–90 dB) showed decreased HRV in response to the loudest version (80–90 dB range) of a heavy metal music excerpt compared with the silent baseline (do Amaral et al., 2015). Mikutta et al. (2013) compared listeners' heart rates during two acoustic recordings (described as rhythmically regular and rhythmically expressive) of a ten-minute excerpt of classical music. Listeners' heart rates were positively correlated with the sound intensity for the rhythmically expressive excerpt; subjective ratings of arousal correlated with the sound intensity as well in this condition. In a study described earlier, Chuen et al. (2016) tested whether sudden shifts in sound intensity from baseline tones (65 dB) to loud tones (70 dB, 75 dB, and 80 dB) in a rhythmic sequence of tones influenced cardiac activity (HR), SCR, and respiration rate. Listeners' heart rates generally increased as the sound intensity increased. Moreover, heart rate showed a fluctuation pattern when tones increased by 10 dB, such that there was an immediate decrease in heart rate followed by a delayed increase in heart rate. SCR showed a roughly proportional change in size to the change in tone intensity (Chuen et al., 2016). Finally, Cheng and Tsai (2016) had females listen to thirty seconds of Soft musical sound (sea wave sounds) and Loud music (heavy metal) that alternated in both orders to create the following conditions: Loud music + Soft musical sound, Loud music + Loud music, Soft musical sound + Loud music, and Soft musical sound + Soft musical sound. Listeners showed increased heart and respiration rates during the loud passage in the Soft + Loud order and decreased heart rate during the soft passage in the Loud + Soft order.

It is perhaps unsurprising that high-intensity music and sudden intensity increases to single tones cause an increased heart rate typical of ANS arousal. In fact, many listeners and concertgoers have likely had this type of experience during a musical crescendo. Increased autonomic arousal with high-intensity music is in line with research into the acoustic startle reflex (ASR), an automatic response to a loud acoustic stimulus that puts an animal in an alert/defence mode (Samuels et al., 2007). The ASR involves not only muscle reactivity but slightly phase-delayed SCR and cardiac response (Turpin et al., 1999), which has been observed by Chuen et al. (2016). Cheng and Tsai (2016) argue for the positive hedonic contrast hypothesis to explain why shifts in music intensity provoke autonomic changes. This hypothesis holds that the response to a particular stimulus is affected by the hedonic (pleasantness) content of a prior stimulus. This hypothesis does not speak to the basic physiology that may be involved in responding to intensity changes in music and also assumes there is hedonic content in the musical stimuli one is hearing, but it provides a potential explanation for self-reports or judgements of music based on their acoustic features such as intensity. Together, the ASR and the positive hedonic contrast hypothesis offer explanations for the effects of musical intensity on physiology.

In summary, musical tempo has a somewhat predictable effect on cardiac and respiratory measures. Fast-tempo music tends to result in increased heart rate, decreased HRV, and increased SCR, providing evidence for weakly coupled cardiac activity in response to a musical tempo (i.e., beat-to-beat heart rates do not match the musical beat in a 1:1 fashion). Effects of slow-tempo music are less clearly established. Some evidence suggests that slow-tempo music decreases heart rate, but some patterns seem to be specific to the direction of tempo change within the music (Bretherton et al., 2019). Inter-individual differences in resting-state physiological variables, particularly heart rate, may differentiate individual listeners' physiological response to the same music tempo and should be considered when choosing musical tempi in a study. Floor effects in heart rates may also contribute to mixed effects of slow music on heart rate; for example, it may be difficult to decrease heart rate significantly below baseline levels, whereas it is easier to increase heart rate above baseline, which may account for the stronger findings for fast-tempo music than for slow-tempo music. Finally, differences between naturalistic stimuli (musical excerpts) and sequences of tones may influence the extent of tempo changes on physiological variables. There is converging evidence that high-intensity music and increases in the intensity of music lead to increases in heart rate, respiration rate, and SCR and decreases in HRV. These changes indicate a general state of increased physiological arousal with a greater sound intensity of music.

Understanding how basic acoustic properties of music, such as tempo and intensity, influence ANS activity and physiological arousal is important for using music as a formal therapeutic intervention, as well as for informing the general public how they might use music to adjust their level of arousal and mood (Saarikallio, 2011). In therapeutic settings, music can be used to address medical procedure anxiety (Wu et al., 2017) and maladaptive physiological responses in psychological and psychiatric disorders (Landis-Shack et al., 2017), or regulate cardiac function in cardiovascular disease (Martiniano et al., 2018). Finally, individual differences in music preferences, such as familiarity, liking, and how the emotional content of a musical piece matches one's current emotional state, have the potential to influence the relationship between musical features of tempo and intensity and physiological variables. The next section addresses these relationships in emotional response to music.

3 Emotional Response to Music

The potential for music to influence or invoke emotions in listeners is well-documented. It is common for individuals to use music to modulate and regulate their moods (Saarikallio, 2011), and many researchers have investigated music-induced emotional experiences (for reviews, see Eerola et al., 2018; Sachs et al., 2015; Swaminathan & Schellenberg, 2015). Although some studies of perceived (as opposed to experienced) emotional content of music have included physiological markers, the majority of recent studies that incorporate physiological correlates of emotion during music listening start from the assumption that listeners feel emotions in response to music. As pointed out by Eerola et al. (2018), how physiological responses correspond to emotional experiences has yet to be completely understood, a point that applies equally to non-music-induced and music-induced emotional experiences. This section describes studies that investigated the relationship among music listening, emotional response, and physiological response.

3.1 Emotional Arousal and Valence

Researchers have investigated how the emotional content of music impacts a listener's psychological and physiological responses by presenting listeners with multiple pieces of music that differ in their valence and arousal levels. Valence refers to the positive (pleasant) or negative (unpleasant) quality of an emotion, and arousal refers to feeling calm or excited (Lang et al., 1997). The two-dimensional circumplex model of emotion holds that emotions can be described along two independent dimensions of valence and arousal (Eerola & Vuoskoski, 2013). Together, these axes form a four-quadrant space, and emotion-invoking stimuli can be categorised into each of the four quadrants: high valence and high arousal, high valence and low arousal, low valence and high arousal, and low valence and low arousal. Positive emotions are typically high in valence. For example, joy is a high-valence, high-arousal emotion; and tenderness is a high-valence, low-arousal emotion. Conversely, negative emotions are typically low in valence. For example, fear is a low-valence, high-arousal emotion; and sadness is a low-valence, low-arousal emotion (Eerola & Vuoskoski, 2013). In many studies that manipulate musical valence and arousal, the selected music pieces are rated on the valence and arousal dimensions in pilot studies or come from large databases of pre-validated songs or musical excerpts. The overarching goal of this research is to examine how manipulating the valence and arousal of a piece of music leads to emotional changes, as indexed by self-reports and ANS activity (HR, HRV, respiration, and SCR), that is thought to reflect an emotional response in an individual.

Studies have investigated whether manipulating the valence and arousal induced by music produces different emotional and autonomic responses in listeners. Bullack et al. (2018) compared emotional and autonomic responses to instrumental music identified in a pilot study as happy or sad. Excerpts were chosen based on pilot study ratings on a four-point Likert scale that identified excerpts as high valence (happy) or low valence (sad). Heart rate, skin conductance, and respiration rate, as well as emotional responses, were recorded while individuals listened to the music excerpts. Listeners self-reported more positive emotions and higher arousal while listening to the happy music excerpts, and more negative emotions and lower arousal while listening to the sad excerpts. Additionally, participants showed increases in SCR and respiration rate during happy music excerpts compared to sad music excerpts. Heart rate did not differ between the high-valence and low-valence music conditions, and there were no effects of sex (female/male) or musical expertise on these findings. Similar observations have also been reported in a series of studies by Krabs et al. (2015) who evaluated emotional (six-point Likert scale) and physiological (HR, HRV, and SCR) responses to short music excerpts intended to evoke a positive valence (fast-tempo tone sequence set to 119 BPM) compared to isochronous tone sequences (neutral emotion), music-like noise (unpleasant emotion), and silent baseline. Overall, the authors found that heart rate and SCR increased and HRV decreased during music listening regardless of its emotional content, but that positively valenced music (fast-tempo sequences) tended to elicit a larger physiological response compared to the isochronous (emotionally neutral) tone sequences. Together, these findings provide some support for the interpretation that positively valenced music has an arousing effect on the ANS (increased HR and SCR, decreased HRV) than neutrally valenced music. This conclusion is also in line with earlier findings from Lundqvist et al. (2009).

Other research has investigated how expressiveness of a musical performance (the way in which the performer interprets the music piece) and musical experience modulate emotional and physiological responses to music. Vieillard et al. (2012) manipulated the valence of musical excerpts by presenting musically trained and untrained listeners with pre-rated happy (major mode, tempo range = 92–196 BPM), sad (minor mode, tempo range = 40–60 BPM), and scary (out-of-key notes, tempo = 44–172 BPM) unfamiliar instrumental violin excerpts. Recordings of each musical excerpt also differed in how expressively they were performed (mechanical, expressive), with expressive performances primarily having faster tempo. Heart rate, SCR, respiration, and self-reported emotional intensity experienced (five-point scale) were measured during music listening. Heart rate increased after listening to scary music; SCR measures did not differ across the music excerpts but were higher for more expressive music performances, partially supporting an arousing effect of emotional music on the ANS. Furthermore, musically trained listeners' emotional responses were more intense for the expressive versions of scary music performances compared to the sad and happy performances; musical training did not distinguish listener groups' physiological response to the sad or happy music excerpts. These findings suggest that some physiological and emotional responses to music are seen across individuals regardless of their musical training, while other emotional responses (involving performance variables) are modulated by musical training.

Studies have also addressed the role that cultural familiarity with musical styles may have on emotional and physiological responses. Egermann et al. (2015) asked Canadians and Congolese Pygmies to listen to both Western music (instrumental orchestral) and Pygmy music (vocal polyphonic), each group being unfamiliar with the other group's musical styles. Furthermore, the arousal level of the musical styles was manipulated (fast versus slow tempo). Heart rate, HRV, SCR, and respiration rate were recorded while individuals listened to the musical excerpts and provided self-reported ratings of felt valence and arousal. Subjective arousal ratings correlated positively with heart rate, SCR, and respiration rate for high arousal (fast tempo) Western music across both groups. Increases in heart rate were correlated with faster-tempo music, and increases in SCR were correlated with higher pitches and faster-tempo music for both groups. Most listeners indicated positively valenced emotional responses during music listening. The listener groups diverged in their physiological response to Pygmy music, with Pygmies showing increased SCR and decreased heart rate during high-arousal Pygmy music and Canadians showing only increased respiration rates during high-arousal Pygmy music. There were no effects on HRV. Egermann et al. (2015) suggest their findings are partially supportive of universal emotional and physiological responses to high-arousal music; the findings are also in line with an arousing effect on the ANS of the positively valenced, high-arousal music pieces. Overall, this study suggests that listeners' physiological responses were associated with emotional experiences during music listening that extended beyond culture-specific musical styles and musical training differences. This is consistent with Vieillard et al.'s (2012) observation that emotional and physiological responses to music may not be strongly modulated by musical training.

The role of familiarity with musical genres in eliciting emotion-linked physiological responses has also been explored in studies manipulating the musical valence and arousal of music. White and Rickard (2016) used previously validated, moderately familiar happy (high valence, high arousal) and sad (low valence, low arousal) musical excerpts and measured heart rate, SCR, and self-reported feelings of happiness and sadness (seven-point Likert scale). Compared to a silent baseline condition, the listeners' heart rate and SCR measures decreased in response to both happy and sad music; emotional ratings showed that the happy music (high valence, high arousal) elicited happier feelings and the sad music (low valence, low arousal) elicited sadder feelings. The listeners' familiarity with the musical excerpts used in the study may have influenced their physiological responses to the musical excerpts in addition to their experienced arousal; however, familiarity was not explicitly tested.

Controlling for the emotional valence of the musical excerpts, Lynar et al. (2017) compared emotional and physiological responses (HR, HRV, SCR, and respiration rate) during a high-valence/low-arousal classical music piece, a high-valence/high-arousal jazz music piece, a self-selected piece of music (uplifting), white noise, and silent baseline. Self-reported emotional responses indicated that joy and engagement were highest for self-selected music and relaxation was highest during the low-arousal classical piece. Heart rate variability was increased during the classical piece (high valence, low arousal) relative to all other conditions, and heart rate and SCR were increased during self-selected music pieces relative to all other conditions, indicators of greater physiological (ANS) arousal. These findings are in slight contrast with previously discussed research as they suggest that emotional and physiological responses may differ for familiar music than for unfamiliar music.

Importantly, there may be a key difference between familiarity with a musical system (e.g., Western tonal music) or style (e.g., jazz, classical music) and familiarity with a specific piece of music; familiar musical pieces are more likely to have learned associations or carry meaning for a listener than are familiar musical styles. This distinction may be akin to the difference between listening to a new song put out by one's favourite musician (familiar style) versus listening to one's favourite song from that musician (familiar piece) that has a pre-established emotional connection. It may be the case that music can evoke emotional and physiological responses in a listener even if that specific piece of music is not familiar to the individual, but that familiarity with a specific piece of music can further modulate a listener's emotional and physiological response.

Together, these studies suggest that listeners' familiarity with specific musical excerpts and with musical styles or genres can influence both emotional and physiological responses to the music. High-valence, high-arousal music tends to elicit positive emotional responses in a listener, and heart rate and SCR increases often accompany these emotional responses which indicates an arousing effect on the ANS. There is also a pattern of faster music tempo correlating with higher arousal emotional and physiological responses. These findings suggest that acoustic properties of specific musical excerpts used may impact listeners' emotional responses in different ways, depending on their familiarity. This topic is discussed in the next section.

3.2 Acoustic Features Affect Felt Emotion and Physiological Response

Many studies have investigated how musical structure and acoustic features are related to emotional responses and accompanying physiological responses. This research posits that our emotional responses to music occur as a result of the acoustic features of a piece of music such as pitch, tempo, or loudness (among others). Some studies leave their explanations as to how music leads to emotional responses at the level of the acoustic features. Other researchers suggest that explanations as to *how* or *why* music produces emotional (including physiological) responses are incomplete without also invoking psychological mechanisms (discussed later in this section) that are sensitive to certain acoustic features of music, which in turn lead to emotional responses (see Juslin, 2013; Omigie, 2016 for reviews). This section will describe studies that have investigated the relationship between acoustic features of music and emotional and physiological responses, as well as potential psychological mechanisms that may be involved in emotional responses.

By presenting musical pieces that vary in their acoustic features, researchers have identified which aspects of music evoke emotion-related physiological changes in listeners. Coutinho and Cangelosi (2011) used nine pieces of instrumental Western art music that varied in their arousal and valence ratings. During each piece of music, listeners reported their own arousal and valence levels, and heart rate and SCR were recorded. Feature extraction was performed on each piece of music for loudness, tempo, pitch level, melodic contour, timbre (sharpness), and texture. Listeners' subjective arousal ratings increased in response to louder pieces, faster tempo pieces, higher pitch range, and greater sharpness (dimension of timbre related to loudness) of the music. Subjective valence ratings increased in response to faster tempi and higher pitches. Heart rate increased during louder musical pieces and was positively correlated with subjective arousal ratings during music listening. SCR did not change in response to listeners' emotional responses or acoustic features of the music. These findings suggest that cardiac activity may be sensitive to certain acoustic features of music (loudness) that influence arousal aspects of emotion rather than valence aspects.

A relationship between acoustic features of music and physiological markers of emotional arousal has also been reported by van der Zwaag et al. (2011). In this study, listeners' heart rate, SCR, and subjective arousal were measured while they heard pop and rock songs that varied in mode (minor/major), tempo (fast, slow), and percussiveness (high/low). Listeners reported higher arousal during fast-tempo music and during minor mode music with low percussiveness. In contrast to Coutinho and Cangelosi (2011), skin conduction responses were more frequent and larger in response to fast-tempo music and highly percussive music, and SCR correlated positively with listeners' subjective arousal ratings. No effects on heart rate were reported.

Another approach to understanding how acoustic features influence emotional and physiological responses is to manipulate individual acoustic features of a single musical chord and observe changes in the emotional and physiological responses. Olsen and Stevens (2013) used single violin chords that varied in the direction of their intensity change (increasing vs decreasing) and their duration (1.8 s, 3.6 s). They asked listeners to rate their arousal and valence responses to the chords and measured SCR. Single chords increasing in intensity produced greater feelings of listeners' subjective arousal than single chords decreasing in intensity and were also perceived as being louder. Skin conductance responses had a longer rise time for increasing intensity chords but showed larger amplitudes for decreasing than for increasing intensity chords. Longer chords (3.6 s) received more unpleasant ratings than shorter (1.8 s) chords (Olsen & Stevens, 2013). The relationship between acoustic intensity, direction of intensity change, emotional arousal, and physiological arousal is less clear, although it is important to keep in mind that no explicit analyses examined the relationship between the subjective emotional reports and physiological responses.

There are notable methodological differences between Coutinho and Cangelosi (2011), van der Zwaag et al. (2011), and Olsen and Stevens (2013), discussed earlier in the text, that may inform the somewhat-discrepant findings. First, two of the three studies used musical excerpts, while the third used simple sequences of violin chords. Second, the participant samples used in the studies varied in their musical experience, ranging from listeners with no musical training to listeners with fifteen or more years of musical training. Research suggests that listeners who score high in musical experience (listening habits and training) have more unpleasant emotional responses to dissonant classical pieces of music than listeners who score low in musical experience (Dellacherie et al., 2011). However, it is worth noting that Dellacherie et al. (2011) did not observe differences in HR or SCR between the high and low experience groups or the dissonant vs consonant excerpts (in line with findings discussed earlier). Third, the musical genre of the excerpts varied between Coutinho and Cangelosi (2011) and van der Zwaag et al.'s (2011) studies. Different physiological responses to acoustic features observed in the studies may be explained by musical preferences, genre familiarity, or the presence/absence of lyrics. Future studies should consider differences and similarities in these variables, to more fully understand how acoustic features may induce emotions and physiological changes. Finally, Olsen and Stevens (2013) observed a general decrease in listeners' SCR over time in their experiment, suggesting a possible physiological habituation effect to the musical stimuli. Studies that employ long musical excerpts or many musical excerpts may be susceptible to habituation effects; physiological responses may be dampened in later trials.

3.2.1 Rhythmic Entrainment Underlying Emotional Response

The rhythmic entrainment of physiological systems to the musical tempo (synchronisation between musical beats and periodic physiological variables), observed particularly in cardiac activity and respiration, has been explored as a potential mechanism for emotion induction (for reviews, see Trost et al., 2017; Vuilleumier & Trost, 2015). An explicit test of the rhythmic entrainment theory of music-induced emotions was conducted by Krabs et al. (2015) by manipulating the musical tempo (fast = 120 BPM and slow = 90 BPM) and the musical valence (high-pleasant or low-unpleasant) while measuring listeners' heart rate and HRV during listening. Listeners reported that the most positive emotions were felt during the high-valence music irrespective of the tempo, whereas they reported that the low-valence music was rated as most arousing irrespective of the tempo. Heart rate and HRV did not differ across the musical tempo or valence conditions. As faster tempo music did not lead to faster heart rates, and slow-tempo music did not lead to slower heart rates, these findings suggest that cardiac entrainment to the music did not occur despite listeners reporting emotional responses to the music (Krabs et al., 2015).

Another study addressed musical features of tempo, mode, and meter by comparing a subjective entrainment questionnaire (the extent to which one feels in synchrony with or entrained to the music) with physiological measurements (HR, respiration rate) and emotional responses (1–5 rating of feeling vitality, sublimity, and unease) (Labbé et al., 2020). The authors varied chord sequences in tempo (fast/slow), mode (A major/A minor), and meter (4/4 or 5/4) and included a randomly structured sequence in 4/4 meter as well. Listeners' heart rates were faster in response to major than to minor chord sequences but did not increase with tempo or metre, while respiration was largely unaffected. Subjective ratings of entrainment were greater with faster tempo music. Higher ratings of the emotion 'vitality' (positive emotion) were related to the major mode and a greater subjective sense of entrainment with the music. This finding suggests that several musical dimensions should be considered in explicit tests of the entrainment hypothesis of music-induced emotions.

3.2.2 Psychological Mechanisms Underlying Emotional Response

Another theoretical framework for understanding how musical features induce emotions and physiological responses posits that several psychological mechanisms serve as the explanatory variable in mapping acoustic features to emotional and physiological responses. Four primary psychological mechanisms in music-induced emotions have been investigated: brainstem reflex, emotional contagion (mimicking of a perceived emotional state), episodic memory activation, and expectation violation. Juslin et al. (2014) created four versions of a single musical excerpt with different acoustic features manipulated across excerpts to activate each of the mechanisms. Emotional contagion was targeted by the main melody being performed by the cello, thought to resemble a human voice. The brainstem reflex was targeted by adding a loud chord during the music excerpt designed to elicit a startle- or vigilance-like response. Episodic memory was targeted by inserting a short excerpt of a familiar theme into the primary musical excerpt. Finally, expectation violation was targeted by decreasing the tonal stability of the piece (transpositions of six semitones), making the progression of the melody less predictable for the listener. Juslin et al. (2014) found that brainstem manipulations produced the highest surprise/astonishment emotions, that emotional contagion manipulations produced the highest sadness/melancholy emotions, that episodic memory manipulations produced the highest happiness/nostalgia emotions, and that expectation violations produced the highest anger/anxiety emotions. Listeners' SCRs increased in response to the acoustic features intended to evoke the brainstem reflex, episodic memory, and expectation violations.

Listeners also reported increased arousal during the music excerpts correspond-
ing to these psychological mechanisms (Juslin et al., 2014). Listeners' heart
rates did not differ across the manipulations of musical features.

Building on these findings, Juslin et al. (2015) conducted a series of studies
using different musical excerpts to target each of the same four psychological
mechanisms (brainstem reflex, emotional contagion, episodic memory activation, and expectation violation). In each study, listeners heard four different
pieces of music (mean excerpt length across studies was seventy-two seconds)
that targeted a specific psychological mechanism as well as one emotionally
neutral music excerpt (duration was fifty-nine seconds). The brainstem reflex
was targeted with loud music containing sharp attacks; emotional contagion
was targeted with music containing a solo cello or violin voice; episodic
memory was targeted with highly familiar musical excerpts; and the expectation
violation mechanism was targeted by excerpts with low key clarity. Listeners
reported feelings of surprise during brainstem-targeted music, sadness during
emotional contagion-targeted music, nostalgia and happiness during episodic
memory-targeted music, and anxiety during expectation violation-targeted
music (Juslin et al., 2015). Skin conductance response was generally greater
during music listening than during a silent baseline but did not appear to
differentiate any of the emotional responses or psychological mechanism
conditions.

Together, these studies suggest that psychological mechanisms may be targeted through certain features of music and these mechanisms are related to
distinct emotional experiences during music listening. On the other hand, no
clear pattern of physiological responses to the musical features emerges from
these studies, suggesting that physiological responses may have been independent of the specific emotional responses targeted by the musical manipulations.
This point is underscored by findings from Egermann et al. (2013) who investigated expectation violation by evaluating listeners' subjective arousal and
valence responses as well as HR, SCR, and respiration in a group setting during
live performances of four instrumental classical music pieces. Moments of low
expectedness (lower pitch predictability) in the musical structure were identified by two independent music theorists as well as by a computational model.
Unexpected musical moments produced greater subjective arousal responses,
but physiological responses were inconsistent with increased arousal. Heart rate
decreased slightly and respiration rate increased slightly during unexpected
musical changes, while SCR increased during both highly expected and unexpected changes in the music. As Egermann et al. (2013) did not systematically
compare musical features or other psychological mechanisms than musical
expectancy, it is possible that other psychological mechanisms or acoustic

features contributed to the divergent physiological responses. Future research is needed to systematically evaluate the relationships between acoustic features and psychological mechanisms implicated in music-induced emotions.

In summary, a number of studies have sought to connect specific acoustic features with physiological responses during emotional experiences. Most notable are listeners' increased SCR in response to faster tempo music and to louder music, and some evidence for greater increases in HR in response to major mode music than to minor mode music. One pattern among these studies is the non-specificity of physiological responses during music-induced emotional experiences. Many studies agree that physiological activity accompanying an emotional response is less an index of a specific emotion than it is an index of general autonomic arousal accompanying an emotional response (Juslin, 2013). More recent theoretical frameworks attempt to account for emotional responses to music by appealing to a set of psychological mechanisms at play during these responses. This framework incorporates psychological mechanisms thought to underpin emotional responses to music. Future research may continue to test explicitly how the psychological mechanisms relate to acoustic features and to the listener's specific emotional and physiological response.

3.3 Pleasure and Chills Response to Music

Listening to music can be a rewarding, pleasurable experience, and several studies have investigated the neural and physiological bases of music-induced pleasure and reward (for reviews, see Belfi & Loui, 2020; Salimpoor et al., 2015; Zatorre, 2015; Zatorre & Salimpoor, 2013). One commonly used correlate of music-induced pleasure is the chills response which has been described as having goose bumps on the skin (Panskepp, 1995) or a shiver down the spine (Blood & Zatorre, 2001). The chills response can be measured objectively by SCR, and it is typically accompanied by a subjective feeling of pleasure as well as increases in autonomic arousal (Blood & Zatorre, 2001; Guhn et al., 2007). Several studies have examined the chills response to music that is familiar to a listener. Research discussed in this section will focus on studies that have used unfamiliar or experimenter-chosen pieces of music, combined with physiological measures, to investigate the chills response.

Several researchers have linked music-induced chills to specific passages and acoustic features of music. Bannister and Eerola (2018) aimed to causally tie music-induced chills to specific moments in a piece of music by presenting listeners with chills-inducing music based on measures of chills-inducing reports collected in a pilot study. The same musical excerpts were then presented to listeners without the segment that elicited the chills response. The frequency with which listeners reported the chill response was slightly higher for the original excerpts than in the chills-removed versions. The listeners' SCR was larger only during the chills section in the original pieces, compared to other structurally similar sections of the music piece. Although the experimentally measured loudness and brightness (pitch height) features of the music correlated positively with the frequency of chills reported, these acoustic parameters did not correlate with the SCR measures.

To explicitly test the role of certain acoustic features in eliciting chills responses, Bannister (2020) investigated whether loudness and brightness changes in a musical piece may lead to music-induced chills in the presence of auditory looming. Auditory looming refers to the perception that a sound increases more in intensity as the sound source approaches the hearer (and is, therefore, more important to attend to) than a sound that recedes in distance from the hearer (Baumgartner et al., 2017). Listeners were presented with two pieces of unfamiliar music previously shown to have sections that elicited chills responses. One piece (154 seconds duration) contained cues to elicit auditory looming (a section of the music with increased dynamics and layering of instruments), while the second piece (104 seconds duration) did not. The sections of the music associated with chills responses were manipulated so that listeners heard five versions of each music excerpt: original version, high loudness, low loudness, high brightness (increased amplitude of frequencies above 2000 Hz), and low brightness (decreased amplitude of frequencies above 2000 Hz). Bannister (2020) found the frequency of chills reports increased when the music contained auditory looming, was loud, and had decreased brightness. However, there was no difference in the intensity or duration of SCR responses between any music conditions.

Together, Bannister and Eerola's (2018) and Bannister's (2020) studies suggest that SCR response to music-induced chills are limited to the musical sections reported to elicit the chills response and are relatively insensitive to manipulations of the musical structure and the acoustic features. In contrast, Tsai & Chen (2015) reported that repetitions of musical themes in classical sonatas tended to elicit listeners' chills as well as increased heart rate and SCR and decreased respiration depth. The authors attributed the physiological responses to a release of tension in the music built up before the theme's recurrence. Crucially, listeners in this study were familiar with all musical excerpts; that is true for many of the studies that report on the chills response to music, and so it is difficult to draw inferences about the role of the musical structure alone in the physiological responses observed.

In addition to considering effects of acoustic musical parameters on self-reported chills responses and physiological responses, researchers have examined the role of cultural experience or musical familiarity in the chills response. Beier et al. (2020) tested chills responses (self-report judgements and SCR measures) in listeners who were familiar with Western classical music and had varying degrees of familiarity with traditional Chinese or classical Hindustani music. In addition to these musical excerpts, scrambled versions of each excerpt were presented that contained the same acoustic features but disrupted the musical structure by randomly reordering 250 ms segments. Beier et al. (2020) found that listeners reported and experienced (based on SCR frequency) a similar number of chills for both culturally familiar and unfamiliar excerpts, but fewer chills in response to the scrambled musical pieces. This suggests that prior knowledge of a cultural music form is not necessary for the chills response to occur; the authors proposed that the structural regularities across the musical cultures (as opposed to just the acoustic features of the music) contributed to the chills response. The importance of acoustic features in structured music for the chills response was, however, supported by a positive correlation between the frequency of listeners' chills responses and the loudness, brightness (high-frequency content), and roughness peaks (high sensory dissonance) in the original excerpts but not the scrambled musical excerpts (Beier et al., 2020). These manipulations suggest that intact musical structure is critical for the effects of acoustic parameters on the physiological response to chills, while familiarity with a musical style is not critical for that effect.

Other studies have tested the chills response using musical styles designed for dance movements. Humans frequently listen to dance music in the presence of others, a point that led Solberg and Dibben (2019) to wonder whether music that is primarily heard in group dance settings, such as electronic dance music, still elicits an emotional chills response when heard in a passive listening setting. Electronic dance music often has a break routine which contains a period of ramped-down musical structure, followed by a build-up period, and finally a drop where the groove of the music returns. Solberg and Dibben had individuals listen to four commercially available electronic dance music tracks, each containing a break routine, and one track without a break routine. Increased SCR responses were positively correlated with self-reported pleasurable feelings during the music and SCRs were largest during the drop period of the music. Additionally, SCR correlated positively with audio amplitude, spectral flux, and brightness of certain tracks. However, acoustic features could not explain the consistent increase in chills response to the drop section of the music. Listeners were not familiar with the excerpts used in the study but generally enjoyed listening and dancing to electronic dance music (Solberg &

Dibben, 2019). The overall structure of electronic dance music (the break routine) may play a role in the chills response in addition to acoustic features.

Researchers have also investigated whether the chills response differs when the music is heard in a solo versus a group listening setting. Egermann et al. (2011) addressed whether emotional responses to music are amplified in group settings, such as music concerts. Egermann et al. (2011) compared listeners' chills responses to recordings of familiar classical music heard in a solo setting and in a group setting in the presence of other (familiar) individuals. Contrary to their predictions, listeners showed larger SCR responses during the solo setting than during the group setting. This finding suggests that emotional chills responses may also depend on the listening setting; the authors suggest that social appraisal of group members and/or attentional factors might influence the findings. Future studies are needed to disentangle the musical and extra-musical factors that contribute to emotional chills responses to music, including distinctions between live music performances and recorded music. The next section focuses on the role of movement during performance, and physiological influences of music.

4 Movement Response to Music

In previous sections of this Element, we described how passive listening to music affects physiology. A strong natural behavioural response to music is to move with its rhythm. Musical rhythm tends to induce motor responses in listeners such as foot tapping, hand clapping, or head bobbing. Performing music also requires the production of very precise movement sequences. Music is thereby intrinsically linked to movement. Several studies address physiological effects of music when motor production is involved. In this section, we first review the physiological changes induced by movement when musicians perform. We also address questions of how coupling of movement to auditory rhythms (entrainment) affects physiology, and how music listening increases exertion and changes physiology during physical activities.

4.1 Performing Music

When performing music on stage, during rehearsal, or simply practicing at home, musicians experience changes in their physical and mental states. For example, performing music can induce a feeling of *flow*, a state of total absorption in an activity (de Manzano et al., 2010). Performing music is a more active, engaging activity than listening to music, and musicians' body movements may elicit different physiological responses that sustain the physical and mental states they experience.

One study (Nakahara et al., 2011) directly addressed the question of how physiological reactions differ in active performance and in performers' passive listening to the same musical material. Cardiac and respiratory activity was recorded as pianists performed or listened to a recording of the same piece of music. The authors also manipulated the emotional intentions of the performances: pianists performed with normal expressive emotions, without emotional expression, or without emotion and increased forte touch, while minimising ancillary body movements. The listening conditions consisted of passive listening to the recordings of the three performance conditions (each participant heard their own performance). Both heart rate and HRV were higher in the performance conditions compared with the passive listening conditions. They were also higher in the emotional expression conditions than the non-emotional conditions; overall, HR and HRV were highest in the conditions in which pianists performed the excerpt with emotional intent. Similarly, reported measures of arousal and pleasant emotions were higher in the performance conditions compared with the passive listening conditions and in the emotional conditions compared with the non-emotional conditions. Finally, oxygen consumption was higher in the performance conditions. Thus, the physiological effects of performing music were manifested in both cardiac and respiratory measures, compared with the same individuals during listening to the same performances. It is possible that the physiological changes observed when performing music are explained by the physiological generation of the body movements necessary to perform. The fact that there was a significant interaction between the task (listening vs. playing) and emotional expression levels (emotional vs. non-emotional conditions) for cardiac measures suggests that the effect of making music is not only due to the movements required in music performance but also due to the expressive intentions of the performers.

Additional studies have addressed the temporal relationship between musicians' breathing and movement during music performance. One study compared pianists' finger movements with their respiration while they played repetitive exercises (the C major scale and arpeggio) at different tempi (60, 80, 120, 160, and 184 BPM) (Nassrallah et al., 2013). There was no alignment between the timing of performers' inspiration and expiration and their arm/finger movements (forearm and finger flexion and extension) suggesting that effects of performing music on physiology may not be explained merely by a coordination between the cardiorespiratory system and the fine motor actions. These results of Nassrallah et al. (2013) are contradictory to another study (Ebert et al., 2002) in which pianists' breathing was coordinated with their arm/finger movements, at least for more challenging music that included complex metres (5/4 or 7/4). Musicians' breathing and movement during performance may therefore appear coordinated when the mental effort is higher.

Another factor influencing physiology is the role of the performers' emotional engagement. The metaphor of performers' flow is used to describe a feeling of perfect harmony and union with one's surroundings while making music. Unsurprisingly, physiological changes are associated with the experience of flow during music performance. De Manzano et al. (2010) asked pianists to play a self-selected musical piece for three to seven minutes. Participants repeated the piece they chose five times, with a one- to two-minute break between repetitions, in order to induce a change in flow. Physiological measures, including cardiac activity via arterial pulse waveform (variation in blood pressure) and respiration, were collected during each repetition, as well as head movements and facial muscle activity. Participants completed ratings of experienced flow after each trial. Results showed that increased ratings of flow corresponded to decreased HR and RSA and increased HRV and respiratory depth (de Manzano et al., 2010). Cardiac output was also associated with flow, with a decrease in blood pressure. The authors acknowledged that the experience of flow in a physically and cognitively demanding task such as performing music is associated with increased activation of the sympathetic nervous system and deep breathing.

Cardiac and respiratory measures have also been investigated during cognitively demanding musical tasks (Harmat et al., 2011). The authors compared cardiorespiratory measures as musicians performed a familiar (self-chosen) piece and an unfamiliar prima vista piece that they sightread from a notated score. Performers showed lower heart rates, higher respiration rate, and lower end tidal carbon dioxide concentration (indicating more pronounced respiration ventilation) during performances of the unfamiliar piece. High-frequency HRV power (indicating high vagal activity) was greater in the first minute of the unfamiliar piece, but this effect was not sustained.

Larger respiratory responses during demanding music performances were also observed in musicians playing wind instruments (Blasco-Lafarga et al., 2020). Participants played pieces that they had previously ranked as mildly difficult (mild performance) and very difficult (difficult performance). They performed each piece on two days for twenty minutes and repeated it two times with a five-minute break between each repetition. HRV was recorded for forty minutes (two twenty-minute repetitions with a five-minute break between them), and before and after the performances. Results showed greater increases in short-term HRV during the difficult performances than the mildly difficult performances, indicating larger parasympathetic responses, but no difference in heart rates (Blasco-Lafarga et al., 2020). The differences observed in physiological variables between the difficult and mild performances were more pronounced during the second repetition of the piece.

Blasco-Lafarga et al. (2020) examined performances on wind instruments (such as clarinet, saxophone, flute), which are an interesting case for the study of physiological influences of music. Wind instruments require performers to blow using specific control of the vocal tract, which in turn influences the cardio-respiratory system. A similar case of music performance that requires deep respiration and precise vocal tract control is singing (Wolfe et al., 2009). When vocalists sing, their respiration rate and amplitude are increased in order to maintain efficient control of the vocal tract and laryngeal coordination (The Oxford Handbook of Singing (2019), and specifically the chapter by Lã and Gill, offers a recent overview of the physiology of singing). Singing affects vocalists' cardiorespiratory functions; respiration rate tends to be slower than normal when singing, and HRV may be coupled to the breathing rate, producing RSA (Vickhoff et al., 2013).

Bernardi and collaborators (2017b) asked novices (without vocal training) to sing familiar songs of participants' preference (singing) and to improvise their vocalisations of free vowel sounds (toning). These conditions were compared with a rest condition and two matched breathing-only conditions (without singing or toning): one in which the breathing was similar to the singing (singing-matched breathing only) and one in which the breathing was similar to the toning (toning-matched breathing only) conditions. Cardiac and respiratory measures were collected in all conditions. Heart rate was faster and HRV (SDNN) increased in the singing and toning conditions (higher in the toning condition), compared with the rest condition. The same effects were observed in the singing and toning matched breathing-only conditions, compared with the rest condition. Low-frequency and high-frequency variability increased and decreased, respectively, during singing and toning compared to rest, and the effect was larger with toning than with singing. The breathing-only condition yielded similar effects in singing but smaller effects in toning. Respiratory frequency decreased while tidal volume and minute ventilation increased in the singing and toning conditions. The singing-matched and toning-matched breathing-only conditions produced the same results on respiratory measures, suggesting that the physiological changes were due to the breathing and not to the production of tones *per se* (Bernardi et al., 2017b).

Some research suggests that cardiorespiratory patterns of individuals syn-chronise when vocalists sing together (Müller & Lindenberger, 2011; Vickhoff et al., 2013). Vickhoff and collaborators (2013) compared cardiac and respira-tory activity when singers hummed a single tone or sang simple songs with regular structure composed of half and quarter notes (a hymn or a mantra). The

HR of participants increased and decreased simultaneously when they sang songs with regular structure. Müller and Lindenberger (2011) showed that synchronisation of HRV and respiration variability was greater between individuals singing in unison (i.e., the same musical pitches and durations) than between individuals singing different musical parts of the same piece. This synchronisation of cardiorespiratory functions is observed in experienced choir singers (Müller & Lindenberger, 2011), as well as non-expert singers (Ruiz-Blais et al., 2020).

As seen in the previous section, most studies of performers' physiological measures used linear analyses of cardiac measures (HR, HRV, respiration rate, etc.), Few studies have investigated cardiac rhythms in music performance with non-linear tools which are better suited for capturing oscillatory music activity and cardiac activity, such as recurrence quantification analyses. In a recent study from the authors' lab, we used non-linear methods of recurrence quantification analysis to study dynamics of cardiac activity during piano performance of familiar and unfamiliar melodies (Wright & Palmer, 2020). Pianists' performances were measured at self-selected tempi at four different times of day (9am, 1pm, 5pm, and 9pm) while cardiac measures were recorded and compared with baseline rest. We observed more predictable cardiac dynamics during music performance in early testing times (9am and 1pm) using two different recurrence quantification analysis indices: determinism (how predictable the series of cardiac intervals were) and laminarity (how much the cardiac intervals repeated in their patterning). The same indices were also higher for unfamiliar melodies than for familiar melodies. Linear analyses showed an increase in HR during music performance compared with baseline but no effect on variability (SDNN). Thus, non-linear analyses revealed complex heart rate patterns that were not captured by linear analyses.

4.2 Entrainment of Exercise Movements to Music

As described earlier, entrainment refers to an oscillatory process that adjusts its period in response to another oscillatory process or system (Bittman, 2021). Musical entrainment can reflect the alignment of listeners' movements and physiological responses with the rhythmic structure of the music, such as the beat. A common application of musical entrainment is to help listeners maintain a regular motor pattern when they perform high-intensity exercises. Damm and collaborators (2020) published a review on entrainment of human movement to auditory rhythms with a focus on neurophysiological mechanisms. The authors concluded that music has an ergogenic effect (it enhances physical performance, stamina, or recovery) that can be explained by the entrainment of the brain's neuronal activity and the mechanics of movement to the musical rhythm or periodic regularity. In this section, we review studies that report physiological changes when movement is entrained to music, especially during tasks consisting in rhythmic movements such as walking, running, or cycling.

Effects of musical tempo on physiological and kinematic measures of walking were investigated in a self-paced walking task. Almeida et al. (2015) tested the effect of two music tempi (90 and 140 BPM) on walkers' physiological measures (heart rate, respiration) in comparison with a non-music walking condition. Note that in this experiment, the subjects were not explicitly instructed to walk at the tempo of the music. The presence of the music influenced the average walking speed; the fast-tempo music generated faster walking speeds, suggesting at least some entrainment of movement speed to the musical beat. There were no influences of musical tempo on the physiological variables and the authors did not test whether or not participants' footsteps aligned with the music. Other studies have shown that when walkers are not instructed to synchronise with heard music, they tend not to pace their steps with music (Leow et al., 2018). It is possible that synchronisation to music is necessary in order to observe physiological changes. Another possibility is that music does not elicit physiological changes during relatively undemanding tasks like walking. Physiological changes elicited by music may appear when the physical task demands are higher.

Several physical activities, such as cycling or running, show a greater impact of music listening on physiology. The respiratory system and the locomotor system are coupled when individuals perform these tasks spontaneously, known as locomotor-respiratory coupling (LRC). Studies have shown that the presentation of rhythmic auditory stimuli (such as a regular metronome beat) stabilizes LRC during cycling (Hoffmann & Bardy, 2015; Hoffmann et al., 2012; for a short overview, see Bardy et al., 2015). Stabilisation of LRC is measured by the ratio between the number of respiration cycles and the number of movement cycles; simple integer multiple values (2:1) are considered more stable. For example, a ratio of one respiration cycle for two movement cycles is considered as stable, whereas a ratio of three to four is considered unstable.

When people walk, cycle, or perform other alternating (periodic) body movements, their physiological patterns (respiration, cardiac activity) tend to be periodic as well. In addition, the musical structure (such as beats and phrases) creates periodic patterns. Thus, non-linear dynamics tools and theories are the most appropriate to capture these patterns. One line of research used a non-linear coupled oscillators model to capture the dynamics of LRC (Bardy et al., 2015; Hoffmann & Bardy, 2015; Hoffmann et al., 2012). Hoffmann et al. (2012) presented an auditory metronome as athletes cycled on an exercise indoor bike that measured the work performed. Participants' preferred locomotor and respiratory rates were first determined, which allowed the researchers to present metronome sounds set equal to either their locomotor rate or respiratory rate. Participants were explicitly instructed to synchronise their pedal cycles with the metronome when it was set to their locomotor preferred rate and to synchronise their breath with the metronome when it was set to the respiratory preferred rate. The presence of the metronome had a stabilisation effect on LRC: more stable frequency ratios between respiration rates and pedaling rates were observed in comparison with a silent condition, such as one respiratory cycle for every two pedal cycles (Hoffmann et al., 2012). They observed stabilising effects of the metronome rates on LRC, observed by reduced oxygen consumption and lower carbon dioxide concentration rates in the music conditions than in the silent condition. This effect was more prominent when the metronome was set equal to the locomotor preferred rate than to the respiratory preferred rate (Hoffmann et al., 2012). In a similar study, Hoffmann and Bardy (2015) used the same experimental set-up, but this time the authors varied the metronome rate to +15% and -15% around cyclists' preferred locomotor and respiratory rates. The stabilising effect of the auditory stimulation on LRC and the decrease in energy expenditure was also observed when the auditory stimulus was faster or slower than the spontaneous cycling rate, compared with a silent a condition (Hoffmann & Bardy, 2015).

Although non-linear dynamic analyses are very powerful, most studies have used linear analyses to study physiological responses when movement is entrained by music. Bacon et al. (2012) used linear analyses to study entrainment of breathing to external sounds. They asked participants to cycle with a fixed number of pedal revolutions per minute (130 half-cycles per minute) while they listened to music that was synchronous to their pedal cycles (130 BPM), slower than (123 BPM) or faster than (137 BPM) the pedal cycles. Participants' oxygen consumption was recorded. The results showed that a reduction of oxygen consumption was observed when the music was synchronous with the pedal cycle, compared with the condition in which the music was slower than the pedal cycle. No significant difference was observed in the condition in which the music was faster than the pedal cycle. This absence of a difference between the synchronised condition and the faster condition might be explained by a lack of statistical power, as only ten participants were included in this study.

Entrainment to music during locomotor activities also affects HR. Waterhouse et al. (2010) asked participants to cycle at a self-chosen rate while they heard six musical excerpts of different tempo. Subjects participated in three twenty-five-minute sessions. Unbeknownst to the participants, the musical tempo was changed in each session. The original tempo of the stimuli was presented in one of the sessions and it was changed by +10% or −10% in the other sessions. Changing music tempo by +10% or −10% increased and decreased HR, respectively, and this was associated with increases and decreases in distance covered/unit time, power exerted, and pedal cadence. Participants were not informed that the tempo of the music changed, and they did not perceive it; entrainment of movement to music may therefore have occurred unconsciously as they may have unconsciously adapted their rate to the tempo of the music.

Bood and colleagues (2013) conducted a related study with treadmill runners who ran to exhaustion in three conditions: with motivational music, with a metronome, and without sound. The authors selected five motivational songs for high-intensity sports, like running at high intensity based on the ratings of a group of students. Runners selected one of the five songs. Music and metronome tempi both matched the frequency of participants' cadence. The authors altered the tempo of the motivational music without changing other aspects of the music using a disk-jockey software. HR was collected every five seconds during the task. The authors also collected ratings of perceived exertion every minute, and time to exhaustion. Time-to-exhaustion measures increased in the music and metronome conditions but did not differ between those conditions. Reductions in perceived exertion and decreased HR were observed in the music condition. The authors attributed this effect to the motivational aspect of the music condition. The absence of differences in time to exhaustion between the music and metronome conditions was an unexpected result. An equivalent beneficial effect of sounded music and a sounded regular beat on time to exhaustion suggests that the effect is due to a reduction in energy expenditure induced by entrainment and not simply to the motivational properties of music.

In a similar experiment with cyclists, Lim and colleagues (2014) tested cyclists' oxygen uptake and HR, ratings of dyspnoea (i.e., breathing discomfort), limb discomfort, affective valence, and arousal, as they listened to music. Three auditory stimulation conditions (synchronous metronome, synchronous music, or asynchronous music) and a silent control condition were included. Participants were told to use the beats of the auditory stimulus to maintain their pedal frequency in the synchronous metronome and synchronous music conditions. HR was lower when participants tried to synchronise with the metronome compared with the asynchronous music and silent conditions, but HR did not differ between the synchronous music condition and other conditions. The authors proposed that the melodic and harmonic qualities present in the music conditions may have masked their physiological influence; the music conditions did, however, elicit more positive affective responses and more arousal.

Di Cagno et al. (2016) further addressed entrainment to music during cycling by testing the effect of fast-tempo musical excerpts (150–170 BPM) in comparison with the same music in which extra-rhythmical elements (melody, lyrics) from the same excerpts were removed. In both conditions, participants reached 75 per cent of their maximum HR more quickly than in a silent control condition, meaning that they increased their training intensity at the beginning of the training session. After reaching this threshold, only the fast-tempo musical excerpts were sufficient to further increase the HR. The authors attributed the lack of differences between the musical excerpts and the rhythm-only music to the motivational benefit that extra-rhythmical elements produced in aiding entrainment to music during exercise (Di Cagno et al., 2016).

Dance is another example of entrainment of movement to music in which the specific properties of music play an important role. Bernardi et al. (2017a) tested the effect of dance movements on cardiorespiratory measures and emotional ratings in non-expert dancers. Participants listened to songs that differed in their *groove*, that is, the degree to which a certain piece of music urges the listener to generate movements. Groovy and non-groovy excerpts were used. Participants improvised movement during the instruction to let their body move freely, inspired by the emotions they felt. Two different control conditions were tested: one in which they listened to the music while standing and refraining from movements and another in which they reproduced the movements they had just produced to music (movement imitation) in the absence of the music. In general, the dancers' movements inspired by groovy music increased their HR and respiratory rate, regardless of the presence or absence of music. In addition, dancers' ratings revealed increased emotional valence when dancing to the groovy excerpts. The analyses also revealed that high-frequency HRV increased during dance to groovy excerpts compared to motor imitation. This effect was not confounded by concurrent changes in respiratory rate, as breathing rates were similar across these two conditions. The authors concluded there was a direct effect of music on physiological markers of emotions (high-frequency HRV) during dancing.

Together, these studies show effects of auditory stimulation on physiological measures (respiration, HR) and on movements, when the musical tempo corresponds in some way to the tempo of one's movements (forming stable ratios such as 1:1 or 2:1). The physiological impact of entrainment of movement to music is seen in reduction of energy consumption. De-synchronisation between tempo and movement may explain the absence of effect observed in several studies (Almeida et al., 2015; Dyer & McKune, 2013). Dyer and McKune (2013) did not observe any effect of music on high-intensity cycling performance.

However, the fastest tempo they used was 140 BPM and the tempi were possibly not sufficient to elicit entrainment. In general, the musical tempo has to be faster during high-intensity training (Di Cagno et al., 2016; Karageorghis et al., 2011; for a review, see Terry et al., 2020) to engage a correspondence between the frequency of the movement at high intensity and the musical tempo.

4.3 Effects of Music on Increased Physical Exertion

In the previous section, we saw that musical tempo can influence both body movement and physiological markers during exercise. Additional variables may also influence physiology and movement during exercise. For example, music can be beneficial when it acts as an extra motivation during long, repetitive efforts as well as for short and intense workouts. It can also divert attention away from the pain induced by physical exertion. In contrast, some types of music can cause a loss of focus for the physical activity and therefore distract from the activity.

In this section, we address how factors such as motivation and arousal are involved in the physiological changes induced by music during motor tasks, including how music can be used to increase exertion. A common physiological measure in physical exercise tasks that push participants to maximal exertion is oxygen consumption (often measured with blood concentration); increased oxygen consumption reflects higher exertion. A meta-analysis on the effects of music on exercise and sports reported that music listening during exercise improved oxygen consumption efficiency, in comparison with no-music control conditions (Terry et al., 2020). Music can also affect other physiological markers in exercise, such as HR, HRV and blood lactate level.

The effect of music on physiological measures of exertion during exercise depends on factors such as the type of exercise, the task, and the tempo of the music. Fast-tempo music can have beneficial effects on heart rate and perceived exertion during low-intensity training (Patania et al., 2020). Patania's goal was to evaluate whether musical tempo could increase exertion in high-intensity training (leg press) compared with low-intensity training (walking). Participants did the two tasks in four different conditions while walking: slow music (90–110 BPM), medium music (130–150 BPM), fast music (170–190 BPM), and a no-music control condition. In the low-intensity condition, fast music reduced the walkers' perception of exhaustion and elicited higher HR than the slow and medium music conditions. Perceived exhaustion and HR were higher in the slow and medium music conditions compared with the non-music control condition. Music also reduced participants' perception of exhaustion in the leg-press condition, and the effect was more pronounced with fast music. The author did not measure HR in the leg-press condition.

Physical activities such as running do not always display synchronisation of movement with music, even when athletes listen to music during their workout. Some studies have shown the physiological arousal effects of music on exertion during workouts. Music affects movement and physiology in aerobic physical activities. Listening to musical excerpts (current Top 40 songs with tempi set to 125–140 BPM) while swimming tends to increase swimmers' speed and HR, compared to a no-music swimming condition (Olson et al., 2015). Participants reported more favourable arousal and affective response in the music condition, although perceived exertion was equivalent to the no-music condition. A related finding from sprint interval training measured HR and power output during a music condition (motivational music; tempo > 120 BPM), a control condition consisting of a 7-minute audio podcast on consumerism devoid of musical qualities, and a silence condition (Stork et al., 2019). Sprinters' HR and power output increased in the music condition compared with both control conditions; post-exercise enjoyment ratings and affective responses were also higher and more positive following the music condition.

Savitha et al. (2013) compared participants who listened to vocal music (containing lyrics) or instrumental music (no lyrics) during a moderate intensity running task and during a silent running task. The music condition showed lower heart rate and oxygen consumption, as well as perceived exertion, and reduced recovery time, compared to a silent condition (Savitha et al., 2013). The music excerpt was the same for all participants, although they ran at different paces; therefore, music was not synchronised. The physiological changes induced by the music were the same whether or not the music contained lyrics. This suggests that the effect is driven by music itself, and not by an additional motivation induced by the lyrics.

A central question is what role motivation plays in exercisers' increased exertion induced by music. Motivational properties of music can be evaluated with the Brunel Music Rating Inventory (BMRI-2), a scale that assesses motivational quality of music during exercise. Terry et al. (2012) compared athletes who ran with self-selected motivational music as well as with neutral music or no music; both music types were evaluated with BMRI-2. The athletes could synchronise their stride to the music with two strides per beat (i.e., tempi ranging 80–97 BPM). Self-reported measures of mood responses and feeling states were more positive with the motivational music. Both types of music proved equally beneficial in lengthening the athletes' time to exhaustion and oxygen consumption compared to no music (Terry et al., 2012). In contrast, blood lactate concentrations were lower only in response to the self-selected motivational music (Terry et al., 2012).

Sometimes motivational music is not sufficient to elicit physiological responses during anaerobic exercise. Rasteiro and collaborators (2020) measured physiological variables (HR, blood lactate) before and after anaerobic threshold intensity training that athletes performed while listening to motivational music or to silence. Each participant provided ten songs which were evaluated with the BMRI-2 scale. The exercise consisted of incremental running tests; there was no synchronisation intended between the movements and the musical tempo. Measures of blood lactate and heart rate increased after training in the presence of motivational music but only for female subjects who increased their total time of effort in the music condition. In a study using an anaerobic test and bench press, Cutrufello et al. (2020) compared athletes who listened to music tracks of songs selected by each participant during the workout (all songs had tempi > 120 BPM), compared with a control condition in which the workout was unaccompanied by music. The total distance covered and the relative peak power (anaerobic test), as well as the number of bench presses, all increased at the same time points in the music condition. Compared with the no-music condition, there was a positive effect of music listening on HR recovery which was reduced two and three minutes after ending the training in the anaerobic test. No effect of music was found during or immediately (one minute) after the training, and the bench press task did not demonstrate changes in physiological measures.

Participants' athletic expertise also influences the effects of musical tempo on exertion. Novice participants (untrained in athletics) completed a high-intensity strength-endurance bout listened to music (band: AC/DC, tempi 94–141 BPM) or worked out with silence. The music had no effect on physiological and psychological measures (heart rate, blood lactate, rate of perceived exertion, perceived pain, and affective reaction) (Brupbacher et al., 2014). The authors found that the participants' work output was reduced in the presence of music, which they surmised may have been because the music was distracting. Another study has shown that trained athletes who listened to music (tempi > 130 BPM) during warm-up and exercises showed increased heart rate and blood pressure and reduced subjective perception of exertion (Arazi et al., 2015), compared with a no-music condition. One possible explanation is that trained athletes can make the movements automatically and be more motivated by the activities without being disturbed by music.

In summary, effects of music on exertion and physiology during exercise have been observed even when music is not synchronised with movement, especially with fast tempi (>120 BPM) (Arazi et al., 2015; Stork et al., 2019). The effect of music depends on various factors such as motivation, the athletes' gender, the type of exercise, and participants' athletic expertise. The findings suggest that music should be tailored to each individual and to the type of physical activity in order to maximise its effect on exertion. An example is the method developed by Fritz and collaborators (2013), in which musical feedback was adapted based on participants' exercise movements while using different fitness machines ('musical agency' condition). The style of the music composition used in the experiment was simplistic electronic (dance) music at 130 BPM. When the musical feedback was adapted to participants' movements, reduced oxygen consumption and perceived exhaustion was observed, compared with a condition where music was not adapted to the exercise movements. Another future direction is the use of interactive music players that can adapt the music based on users' walking and running tempi (such as d-jogger, Moens et al., 2014). Physiological effects of music are recognised by sport associations, as music played by portable music players with earbuds or headphones is often banned in sports competitions (Van Dyck & Leman, 2016). However, music can be used legally in competitive sports during warm-up (Arazi et al., 2015; Chtourou et al., 2012) or during recovery (Cutrufello et al., 2020) where it also has beneficial effects on physiology, such as cardiac and respiratory measures or blood lactate.

In this section, we presented the physiological changes induced by movement when musicians perform. We also addressed the questions of how music listening affects physiology during physical activity. While we have highlighted specific effects, it is important to note that several factors related to the characteristics of the music (tempo, familiarity, genre, etc.), the motor task (instrument played, intensity of the exercise, etc.), and the participants (expertise, gender, motivation, etc.), influence the impact of music on physiology during motor activities. More research that takes a comprehensive, controlled experimental design is needed to further understand the factors that contribute to physiological responses with movement to music. A dynamical systems approach that emphasises non-linear analyses of periodicities has proven fruitful for understanding musical structure and body movements (Scheurich et al., 2018), and is also appropriate for periodic changes in pianists' cardiac activity (Wright & Palmer, 2020). Human-produced music and physiology are intrinsically complex systems with subtle dynamic variations whose periodic components may be fully captured only with non-linear analyses. More efforts in future work should be made to use non-linear dynamics tools (Hoffmann & Bardy, 2015; Hoffmann et al., 2012).

5 Pain Response to Music

One way that people use music in everyday life is to counteract the influences of noxious mental or physical experiences, including painful events that arise from physical exertion or from medical procedures. Many individuals use music as a distraction from painful events, such as listening to one's favourite music during medical procedures, as well as helping to focus their thoughts and reduce stress. Recent studies have investigated the use of music as a non-pharmacological intervention for pain. The use of music to decrease pain intensity or to reduce the need for medications offers the advantages of safety, low to no cost, and ease of application. This combination of features makes music an ideal alternative treatment for pain in children and adults for whom pharmacological treatments come with risks. Several reviews suggest that music listening provides some reduction of experienced pain intensity (Hartling et al., 2009; O'Toole et al., 2017), but the specific features of effective music have not been determined. We review in the next section the experimental application of music listening as a behavioural alternative for reducing experienced pain levels in three settings: (1) recovery following exhaustion from exercise; (2) induced pain in experimental settings and medical procedures; and (3) experienced pain in at-risk newborns in the intensive care unit.

Several physiological markers change with perceived pain. Pain sensation arises both from aspects of the noxious input to peripheral nerves and from the central modulation of that input by factors such as affect, experience, or personality (Cowen et al., 2015). Because the experience of pain differs across individuals, the gold standard of subjective pain is self-reports by adults and children. In the absence of verbal report, as in young infants (covered in the next section), objective measures – both physiological and behavioural – are used to diagnose pain. Physiological markers of self-reported pain include mean HR, HRV, blood pressure (BP), galvanic skin response, and pupil dilation (Cowen et al., 2015). Increased mean HR and HRV are often correlated with increased self-reports of pain and are believed to mark interactions between the sympathetic and parasympathetic nervous system. These physiological variables are also influenced by other factors than pain, including music listening (see Section 1). Noxious stimuli also induce small rises in BP, followed by increased mean HR. Galvanic skin response measures increase as a function of sweating, a common autonomic nervous system response to noxious stimuli, which reduces the skin's electrical resistance and increases its conductance. Sweating is not unique to pain, though, and environmental factors can influence its association with increased GSR. Finally, pupil dilation increases in response to transient (acute) noxious stimuli. However, a variety of factors (including medications) influence pupil dilation in addition to pain. For a review of additional markers of pain, see Cowen et al., 2015.

5.1 Music Affects Recovery from Physical Exhaustion

When individuals switch from an intensive workout to a cool-down period, they often adjust the music to which they are listening, to aid their physiological return to baseline (pre-exertion) levels. Although the effects of music listening on HR factors during exercise have been well-researched (see Karageorghis & Priest, 2012a, 2012b; Terry et al., 2020 for reviews), there has been less consideration of music's effects on the recovery period that follows high levels of physical exertion. High-intensity exercise, defined as >= 70 per cent of aerobic capacity, usually yields laboured breathing, accumulated lactic acid in muscles causing physical discomfort, and fatigue (see Terry, 2020). The recovery period following exercise has been defined as the return of physiological measures (typically HR, pulse, and BP) to baseline or resting state (Karageorghis et al., 2018). Some studies distinguish between active recovery (in which participants perform a non-demanding task such as walking at a self-determined pace) and passive recovery (in which participants remain still, such as sitting). Active recovery in tasks such as low-intensity walking leads to increased blood flow to exhausted muscles which can promote a faster return to homeostasis, including blood lactate levels, compared with passive recovery (complete rest). A few studies of intensive exercise to physical exhaustion have investigated the use of music to hasten or shorten the recovery period following exercise, testing the hypothesis that music plays a recuperative role from a negative valence often associated with physical exhaustion.

Studies have been conducted with presentation of music to runners recovering from an intense six-minute treadmill run at levels of peak oxygen uptake. Eliakim et al. (2012) presented stimulating moderate-tempo dance music (140 BPM) during active recovery from exercise while measuring blood lactate, HR, and perceived exertion. Music listening during a fifteen-minute active recovery walk, compared with no music, was associated with greater movement (number of steps), greater decrease in blood lactate percentage, and greater decrease in perceived exertion, but no differences in HR (Eliakim et al., 2012). To address whether music serves as a distractor, or alternatively arouses a motor response through the rhythmic pattern of the music, the authors conducted another study (Eliakim et al., 2013) in which participants ran on a treadmill at peak oxygen uptake for six minutes, and then walked for fifteen minutes in the active recovery period. During recovery, participants heard (in different conditions) motivational dance music (140 BPM) or only the rhythm beats derived from the same songs (at the same tempo and loudness as the original music). A third condition presented no music during recovery. Hearing music during recovery resulted in a greater number of steps, lower blood lactate levels, and a greater decrease in perceived exertion, compared with no music. The rhythm-only recovery condition also showed increased number of steps and lower blood lactate levels compared with no music. Mean HR did not differ across conditions, similar to other findings (Tan et al., 2014) that music during recovery does not influence mean HR in a study of a four-minute treadmill exercise followed by soothing music or silence during a fifteen-minute passive recovery period (seated). Eliakim et al. (2013) proposed that the rhythm-only condition exerted similar effects as the original musical excerpts on runners' active recovery because the rhythmic features of both conditions were responsible for arousing a motor response.

Other studies have addressed the role of musical tempo on recovery from exertion in aerobic tasks such as treadmill walking and running. Savitha and colleagues (2010) measured the effect of music and tempo on post-exercise recovery time in treadmill walkers who rated their physical exertion. During a passive recovery period following exercise, participants heard slow-tempo songs (< 100 BPM), fast dance music (> 200 BPM), or silence, until their pulse and blood pressure values returned to pre-exercise levels (tempo ranges for slow and fast music and presence/absence of lyrics were not reported). Listening to slow music reduced the amount of time until pulse and perceived exertion values returned to resting levels following exertion, compared with the other conditions. Lee and Kimmerly (2016) compared the effects of self-selected slow-tempo music (60–80 BPM) with a static noise recording on runners' passive recovery following twenty minutes of treadmill running. In addition to manipulating the recovery music, the authors presented fast-tempo music (125–145 BPM) or the static noise during the exercise period. Individuals who listened to slow musical excerpts during recovery showed faster HR recovery and return to blood lactate levels than during static noise, with no difference in ratings of perceived exertion. The reduced HR during the recovery period with slow music was attributed to increased cardiac parasympathetic reactivation, consistent with Bernardi et al. (2006). A caveat to these findings is that the music conditions during exercise and recovery conditions were not fully crossed in the experimental design.

In one of the few studies to compare fast, slow, and no music during recuperation from exhaustive exercise, Karageorghis et al. (2018) measured affective arousal and valence, salivary cortisol, HR, and BP before and after cycling exercise. Participants then performed a three-minute slow cycling active recovery period followed by a passive thirty-minute recovery during which the same measures were taken. Slow-tempo music (mean of 71 BPM) heard during recovery showed the most decrease in affective arousal and lowest salivary cortisol levels, consistent with an expectation that intensive exercise leading to exhaustion causes a sharp change in negative valence, combined with high psychomotor arousal. Fast-tempo music (mean of 129 BPM) elicited the least decrease in HR during recovery. The lack of HR and BP effects of slow music during recovery are somewhat contradictory to findings of Desai et al.'s (2015) study which used a three-minute Harvard step test (typically performed at thirty steps/m) followed by a passive recovery period lasting until HR and BP returned to pre-exercise levels. In their study, the slow-tempo music condition (unreported tempo values) showed a faster return to pre-exercise levels in HR, pulse rate, and BP measures than the fast music or no-music conditions; perceived arousal measures were not taken. It may be that Karageorghis et al.'s (2018) findings pertain to a higher maximal exertion level that is usually accompanied by lower valence and higher arousal than the moderate exercise conditions of Desai et al. (2015). This interpretation is also consistent with studies implicating affective arousal and emotional valence in physiological response to music (see section 3.1).

Recovery from exertion following interval training, which imposes different physiological stresses from those in the previous studies, is another area of recent focus. Interval training intersperses intensive work intervals with rest periods, as is common in several team sports (football, hockey) where the ability to recover quickly between intensive bouts is critical. Furthermore, interval training allows us to consider whether briefer periods of music listening influence upcoming exercise. A common interval training method is high-intensity interval training (HIIT), which is often alternated with brief periods of recovery. Jones et al. (2017) hypothesised that listening to slow-tempo music during the short recovery periods would facilitate cardiac and respiratory recovery when alternated with HIIT, compared with fast-tempo music and no music. Participants performed 5 × 5-minute bouts of treadmill running interspersed with 3-minute periods of standing passive recovery during which they heard slow-tempo music (55–65 BPM), fast-tempo music (125–135 BPM), or no music. Mean HR during recovery indicated lowest values in the no-music condition, and higher values in the fast-tempo condition than the slow-tempo condition. Music conditions did not influence respiratory frequency, blood lactate, or oxygen uptake during recovery periods. Runners' reports of pleasantness during recovery yielded higher values in the fast-tempo music than in other conditions. The authors note that as music was interspersed with physical intensity, effects of musical tempo may be specific to the context: that is, one in which runners were preparing for an upcoming high-intensity event.

Another interval training study addressed the influence of slow, fast, or no musical tempo during recovery periods interspersed with a high-intensity task (Hutchinson & O'Neil, 2020). Participants cycled in a Wingate anaerobic test (WANT) that entailed pedaling as fast as possible for thirty seconds against a braking force adjusted to the participants' body mass. Two high-intensity intervals were interspersed with a ten-minute self-paced cycling recovery time during which participants heard the music. Physiological measures were taken during the ten-minute recovery period and during a final recovery period after the last high-intensity interval. Blood lactate levels increased in the post-recovery period following the slow-tempo music and decreased following the fast-tempo music. Participants in the fast-tempo condition showed higher mean HR during the self-paced recovery periods than in the other music conditions. These findings were consistent with Eliakim et al.'s (2012) findings that fast music during active recovery aids lactate clearance. They are not consistent, however, with Eliakim et. al's finding that fast-tempo music yielded a higher mean HR during recovery. Hutchinson and O'Neil (2020) proposed that a different (unmeasured) variable may have influenced the blood lactate metabolism, such as respiratory rate which tends to increase with HR.

Several important methodological variables distinguish these studies of music's effects on recovery from physical exhaustion, including the use of tasks that generate maximal or sub-maximal exertion levels, the tempo levels of the musical excerpts (sometimes varying across studies or uncontrolled), attentional measures to ensure that listeners perceived the music, listeners' music preferences and/or familiarity, and comparisons of physiological variables with behavioural measures of affective arousal or valence. With these caveats, the majority of findings suggest that listening to slow-tempo music can reduce the recovery time for cardiac (HR, BP) and stress (salivary cortisol) physiological measures, relative to fast-tempo music, static noise, and/or no music. Future directions of interest may include gender-related differences, based on intriguing results (Karageorghis et al., 2018) that women may have different psychological and physiological responses to music during recovery from exertion (in particular affective arousal and cortisol levels), compared with men. Although there are no reviews to date that focus on the use of music for recovery from physical exertion, some reviews address the effects of music listening on recovery from other physical stressors such as medical interventions, the topic of the next section.

5.2 Music Affects Induced Pain

Pain is a fundamental response to noxious stimuli and therefore is considered critical to human evolution by promoting the avoidance of hazardous events.

Pain management is complicated by the fact that pain is a complex subjective experience; people show large individual differences in pain sensitivity and thresholds. Due to these individual differences, combined with pharmacological effectiveness and safety concerns, music as a non-pharmacological treatment for pain has become of great interest. Often referred to as 'music-induced analgesia', several studies have addressed the role of music listening as an alternative treatment for both chronic pain (often arising from long-standing health issues) and for induced pain (arising situationally, during a medical procedure or in an induced laboratory experiment). Early studies focused on the role of music and relaxation in treating induced pain (Roy et al., 2008) but not as much focus was given to physiological markers of pain. This section reviews the scientific evidence for music's effects on physiological variables in pain-inducing contexts: first we consider laboratory-induced pain, and then pain related to medical procedures.

5.2.1 Experimenter-induced Pain

Studies of music listening during experimenter-induced pain typically use a cold pressor test (soaking an arm in a bucket of ice water until some pain threshold is reached) or an intracutaneous (electrical) signal delivered to a fingertip as a constant electric current. Each of these methods is titrated to individual pain sensitivities, by presenting stimuli of increasing intensity until the participant indicates they first feel slight pain (called the pain threshold) and until they report they cannot tolerate higher stimulation (called the pain tolerance).

Using the intracutaneous stimulation method, Bradshaw et al. (2011) simultaneously induced pain while presenting participants with a musical task in which they had to track a familiar melody presented against a distracting auditory background and identify incorrect notes in the melody. Bradshaw et al. (2011) proposed that the role of music as a pain-reducer depends not simply on attention or distraction, but instead on absorption in a task; he proposed that individuals predisposed to become easily absorbed would respond more favourably to music presented during pain than non-absorbed individuals. The music task difficulty was manipulated by changing the relative amplitude (loudness) of the melody and the background sound. In addition, the noxious stimulus was presented at three intensity levels: low (20 per cent of individuals' pain threshold); medium (50 per cent of pain threshold) and high (80 per cent of pain threshold). Skin conductance and pupil dilation responses, and measures of anxiety and absorption were taken as the participants performed the listening task. As the melody listening task increased in difficulty and the noxious stimulus increased in intensity, the skin conduction measures tended to increase. This effect was modulated by participants' reported anxiety level and degree of absorption in the task. Similar complex interactions between the listening task difficulty, stimulus intensity, and perceived anxiety and absorption were found for pupil dilation responses. A weakness of this study is the lack of perceived pain ratings, which the experimenters avoided so as not to influence participants' anxiety and absorption ratings. This is one of the few studies to modulate physiological measures directly by manipulating the difficulty level of the music listening, a promising technique for titrating listeners' attention to the music.

Only a few studies have recently investigated whether music preferences modulate effects of music on pain response. Garcia and Hand (2016) used the cold pressor test to induce pain in participants who listened to self-selected examples of relaxing music, motivating music (assumed to be more stimulating than the relaxing music), or a silent control. Perceived pain was significantly lower after listening to the self-selected relaxing music than during silence. Interestingly, participants rated the motivating music as most preferred; interviews suggested that motivational music was more successful than relaxation music in distracting participants from the noxious stimulus. However, physiological variables of pulse rate and BP taken immediately before and after the cold pressor task did not differ across music conditions, despite the fact that pain unpleasantness ratings were significantly lower for the relaxing music. This finding is exemplary of the fact that musical preferences may modulate effects of music on perceived pain in ways different from their influences on physiological response.

5.2.2 Pain Induced by Medical Procedures

A variety of medical procedures known to induce acute pain responses in patients have been investigated, including dental procedures, surgery, gynecologic procedures, and dressing changes in burn patients. An advantage of pain studies that focus on medical populations is the avoidance of scientific limitations of experimentally induced pain. In particular, experimentally induced pain is transient due to the fact that participants know they can stop the experiment at any time, which may change the experience of pain induced in the lab setting.

Effects of music listening on perceived pain were examined before, during, and after endodontic root canal procedures in patients who received a local anaesthetic (Santana et al., 2017). Patients heard either classical piano music presented in a slow tempo (by Schumann) or silence before, during, and after the procedure. Patients who heard music showed a decreased HRV (SDNN) and decreased low-frequency HR variability during the endodontic treatment compared with the recovery period; patients who heard silence did not show these reductions. Santana et al. (2017) hypothesised that dopamine release in the striatal system, an important neurotransmitter that regulates the autonomic nervous system, was induced by the 'cheerful' music used in the study, and recommended that soothing music be used to reduce cardiovascular responses during painful procedures. No measures of perceived pain, however, were included.

Several studies have introduced music to reduce perceived pain and anxiety in patients during or following surgical procedures. Lee and colleagues (2017) assessed the impact of thirty minutes of music listening for patients in recovery post-surgery following a spinal anaesthetic. One group received the music; the other group received no music (control). In this study patients were offered a choice of six musical styles which they heard prior to surgery. Behavioural indices of anxiety (using the State-Trait Anxiety Inventory) and physiological indices were measured at the beginning of recovery and every five minutes during the thirty-minute period. There were no group differences pre-surgery in mean HR, respiration rate, or BP. Behavioural measures of anxiety (STAI) were significantly lower post-surgery for the music listening group than the control group. The physiological indices of mean HR and respiration rate showed modest but significant decreases in the experimental group post-surgery compared with the control group. In a similar design by the same research team, alert patients undergoing craniotomy procedures listened to music during the entire procedure (Wu et al., 2017); soothing music was chosen beforehand by the participants. Heart rate, respiration rate, and BP were measured before and during the procedure in the music intervention group and in a control group that received the same medical procedure but no music. The music intervention group showed lowered state anxiety (measured with the STAI), lowered HR, and lowered systolic and diastolic BP compared with the control group. The authors proposed that the slow rhythms of the preferred music chosen by patients may account for reduced activity of the autonomic nervous system; however, the musical tempo was not reported for the excerpts used.

As in the previous section on laboratory-induced pain, musical preferences are believed to impact the perception of pain in medical procedures. Self-selected music has generated lower ratings of perceived chronic pain than experimenter-chosen music (see Garza-Villarreal et al., 2017 for a systematic review of chronic pain). Pain is a common symptom of burn victims; the pain arises from tissue damage, from subsequent inflammation, and from dressing changes for the treatment of wounds. Patients report that the dressing changes are considered the most painful time of treatment (Mendoza et al., 2016) and the pain as sharp and intense. Thus, the use of music during dressing changes provides an especially challenging case. Lima et al. (2017) assigned burn patients (94 per cent of which had second degree burns) to three groups: one heard music for thirty minutes prior to the dressing change; the second group heard music for thirty minutes during the dressing change; and the third group heard no music. The music was selected in advance by the patients. All groups received routine analgesia thirty minutes prior to the dressing change. Perceived pain and physiological measures were measured before and after the dressing change when participants reported on perceived pain during the dressing change. All groups reported increased pain during the dressing change and decreased pain following the dressing change. Only the group that heard music during the dressing change reported reduced pain relative to the control group. Mean HR was reduced, and blood oxygenation was increased in the two music groups post-dressing change but not in the control group. These findings reinforce the view that music can confer small physiological changes even when perceived pain benefits are limited.

Music's effects during preoperative periods (often a time of peak anxiety) can also influence physiological states. Labrague and McEnroe-Petitte (2016) investigated music's effects on women undergoing gynaecological surgical procedures; this population was of special interest due to reports that female patients tend to experience higher anxiety levels while undergoing medical procedures, which can in turn influence postoperative outcomes (Caumo et al., 2001; Mitchell, 2003). Participants were assigned to either a music condition or a silent control condition. Participants in the music condition chose from the following three types of sound: classical music (54 per cent), country music (27 per cent), or nature sounds (19 per cent), all chosen to have slow tempo (60–80 BPM), low pitch range and volume, and simple rhythm, intended to be soothing (not arousing). The experimental group listened to music for twenty minutes prior to surgery while the control group did not. Both anxiety measures (STAI) and physiological measures were taken before and after the twenty minute period prior to surgery in both groups. The two groups did not differ on behavioural or physiological measures at the first time point. Comparisons between Time one and Time two (twenty minutes later) indicated that only the experimental group who listened to music showed reductions in anxiety, pulse rate, SBP, and DBP from Time one to Time two. In contrast, the control group showed increased anxiety and pulse rate from Time one to Time two. The authors propose that music may affect sympathetic nervous system activity which in turn decreases HR, pulse, and BP. One of the few studies that included a large sample of female patients, the authors' findings are consistent with other studies described here that show similar effects of music on physiological measures with male and female patients.

Despite the relatively modest benefits of music listening on pain perception and on physiological measures, music has become a popular intervention technique for painful medical procedures, due to its ease of use, low cost, and lack of negative side effects. Reviews of music's impact on chronic conditions such as cancer (Bradt et al., 2016), as well as acute pain in perioperative settings (Nilsson, 2008; Wang et al., 2020) have shown small but consistent relationships between music listening and reductions in some combination of mean HR, respiration rate, pulse rate, and/or BP values, usually accompanied by small reductions in perceived pain. Although the studies often differ on which physiological variables decrease and whether perceived pain decreases, the findings tend to be consistent in the direction of change (downwards) when the music is chosen by the participants and/or the choice is of soothing music (slow tempo, lower amplitude, slow rhythms).

5.3 Music Affects Pain in Neonatal Infancy

In contrast to the fast-tempo music used during exercise, individuals usually turn to slower-paced music in order to sooth or reduce physiological arousal. Music with slower tempo and lower intensity is often used to soothe infants. Parents and other caretakers use music across cultures to soothe babies when they express discomfort. Preterm infants (defined as birth prior to thirty-seven weeks' gestation) in particular are vulnerable to increased pain levels. They account for about 11 per cent of the world's births and have significantly high mortality rates as well as neurodevelopmental consequences. Preterm neonates (infants in the first twenty-eight days of life) are often treated in a neonatal intensive care unit (NICU). Life in an NICU involves regular (daily) exposure to pain-inducing procedures such as heel pricks to obtain blood, IV insertions, injections, and tracheal tubes, as well as to painful environmental stimuli including bright lights and loud noises from machines. Both behavioural and physiological responses to these noxious stimuli are commonly recognised in preterm infants, who make up the majority of cases treated in an NICU. Furthermore, parental access to infants is often restricted during NICU stays; non-human animal research suggests that parental care within the first days of life can lower the stress hormone response (shown in cortisol levels) later in life (for a review see Champagne & Curley, 2009). Due to these factors, there has been great interest in the health care community on the use of music to improve physiological outcomes and behavioural states for these preterm infants who spend 2–3 weeks in the NICU on average, providing a rare opportunity for implementing a music intervention in early development.

Some reviews of pain in preterm infants in the NICU (Pölkki & Korhonen, 2012) have documented music listening's short-term effects on physiological measures of the infants' stress response, including increased blood oxygenation, reduced HR, and decreased respiration and pulse. These studies use a variety of music, including recorded music and live song. Other reviews (Hartling et al., 2009) have reported similar short-term effects of music listening on full-term babies undergoing painful medical procedures, but in only a limited number of the studies reviewed. There has been little investigation of what aspects of music have the most influence on infants' pain reduction. This is an important question, as the newborn infant's auditory system is well-developed by birth and certain musical forms such as lullabies (that typically have slow to moderate tempo and simple rhythms) are used commonly by caretakers to sooth infants (see Trehub et al., 2015 for a review). We review here studies that manipulate the type of music presented to at-risk infants in the NICU during pain-inducing procedures.

Several studies have focused on the effects of Mozart's music on preterm infants, following the finding that adults who listened to Mozart's music performed better on temporal-spatial reasoning tests (Rauscher et al., 1993). This finding was later shown to be modulated by the degree of physiological arousal elicited by the music's tempo, rhythm, and mode (major/minor) characteristics (Thompson et al., 2001). Cavaiuolo et al. (2015) compared preterm infants' pain and physiological response before, during, and after a heel prick when they heard a violin concerto of Mozart (an Adagio, at a slow to moderate tempo) or no music. After the heel prick procedure, the infants in the Mozart condition exhibited decreased HR, increased blood oxygenation, and decreased pain perception (based on the Premature Infant Pain Profile, PIPP), compared with the control group. Amini et al. (2013) compared effects of sung lullaby and a Mozart piano sonata on preterm infants' physiological and pain perception responses. Each infant was exposed for two days, twenty minutes per day to each of the three conditions: folklore lullabies by a young female singer, a Mozart piano sonata, and no music; parents were not present during these interventions. The infants' physiological measures were taken before, during, and after the intervention phase. The infants did not differ in physiological measures before the three interventions. During the interventions, mean HR showed reduction and RR intervals showed lengthening for lullaby and Mozart groups, and this finding increased during post-intervention for the lullaby group; oxygen saturation did not change across treatment groups or testing time.

Some studies have employed music that mimics the infant's auditory environment in the womb. Shabani et al. (2016) presented preterm infants with music in one condition and no sound in the other condition; the condition order was blocked in this within-infant music intervention. The music was presented before, during, and after a heel prick procedure, while physiological markers were measured throughout and infants' facial expressions were recorded. The music was based on a mix of a song sung by an adult female combined with sounds recorded from the uterus of a pregnant woman using an ultrasonic Doppler, chosen to mimic the newborns' sound environment prior to birth. The infants showed similar physiological responses across conditions before the heel prick. Mean heart rates were significantly lower five minutes after the medical procedure for the music condition than for the control condition. Furthermore, ratings of infant facial expressions (based on video recordings) showed lower pain responses following the music condition than the control condition.

Other studies have tested music interventions during more noxious or prolonged medical procedures, including intubation and insertion and removal of tubes for continuous airway pressure machines. Tang and colleagues (2018) assessed the effects of lullabies and nursery rhymes chosen for their slow tempo and simple rhythms in preterm infants who underwent intubation while listening to the music or to no music. Infant pain scores, based on the PIPP scale, were similar for the two groups prior to intubation. The music group had lower pain scores following intubation than did the control group. Mean heart rate decreased and oxygen saturation levels increased for the music group post-intubation, compared with the control group. In addition, blood cortisol levels increased for the control group during and after the intubation but not for the music group. Importantly, the intubation process took less time for the infants who heard music than the control group. Although it was not specified whether the medical staff were blind to the infants' assignment to music/control groups, the authors suggested that music may serve as a successful focus for infants during especially noxious procedures such as intubation.

In a related study, Tekgündüz et al. (2019) assigned preterm infants to one of three groups who received lullabies, a single dose of glucose (a common reward given to neonates before painful medical procedures), or no intervention, while nasal continuous positive airway pressure tracheal tubes were removed and reinserted (a procedure known to invoke pain in infants). Infants' peak HR, oxygen saturation, and facial recordings were collected before, during, and after the medical procedure in this double-blind design. Again, no differences were noted between groups before the medical procedure. The Pain scores (based on the PIPP) of the control group were significantly higher after the medical procedures than those of the other two groups. Peak HR and oxygen saturation did not differ across groups after the medical procedure. Overall, this study suggests that music is as effective for pain management as glucose in preterm infants.

Fewer studies have been conducted with full-term newborns (not treated in an NICU) who hear music while receiving a medical treatment; this population is of interest as it is possible to disentangle infants' pain responses due to medical procedures from those due to hyperstimulation effects of the NICU environment. Rossi et al. (2018) presented healthy newborns with one of three sound conditions shortly after a painful medical procedure (an intramuscular injection or a blood draw screening test). The sound presented was one of three types at a moderate tempo with a regular rhythm: piano music by Mozart, by Beethoven, or heartbeat sound recordings (at 70 BPM). A fourth control group received no sound. The infants heard the music once during the first three days of life, presented for twenty minutes after the medical intervention. Heart rate, oxygen saturation, and pain perception were measured before, during, and after the medical procedure. All groups showed increased HR, decreased oxygen saturation levels, and increased pain (based on the Neonatal Infant Pain Scale) from before to during the medical treatment. After the procedure, the three experimental groups showed faster and larger amounts of recovery than the control group on HR, oxygen saturation, and perceived pain levels. Rossi et al. (2018) suggested that the reason that heartbeat recordings lowered the stress response as much as the music recordings was attributable to the simplicity of the rhythm and its moderate tempo, typical of lullaby-like songs commonly sung to children. The authors also hypothesised that the response to the recorded heartbeat is a familiar stimulus to newborns who are exposed to the maternal heartbeat for several weeks in the womb, after the auditory system is formed.

In sum, a wide range of music applications during medical procedures with preterm infants suggests that music provides a small but consistent advantage in pain relief that tends to (but not always) be accompanied by reduced HR, higher oxygen saturation, and reduced cortisol levels. The size of the effect for music on infants' experienced pain seems comparable to that of a single dose of glucose but larger than no intervention at all; the advantage of music is that it can be continuously applied during procedures of varying durations. Manipulations of musical dimensions suggest that slower tempo, simple rhythms, and repetition provide the most effect, although these dimensions have not yet been manipulated at the same time in the same study. Most studies presented music to infants over speakers placed inside their crib; not every study reported whether medical personnel applying the noxious procedures heard the music, which may have influenced their interactions with the infants. Future directions for research may include controls for whether the infants' parents and the medical staff hear the music, and thus know which condition the infants are assigned to. Additional variables include the roles of musical familiarity and musical preference (especially with respect to tempo), possible impact of the female vocal range (similar to the maternal vocal range), and timbral aspects of music for reducing stress response during pain experienced by infants.

6 Conclusions

This Element provided an overview of physiological responses to music in passive listening and performance/movement settings, with a focus on autonomic nervous system responses (cardiac activity, respiration, electrodermal activity). We reviewed evidence that music perception, in the absence of any task, influences cardiac activity, skin conductance, and respiration. As Table 1 shows, the majority of research published in the past decade has focused on cardiac and respiratory measures during music perception and/or performance. Additional measures to be pursued in future studies include pupil dilation, as well as cortisol measures of physiological arousal. Table 1 also shows that tempo and intensity are common musical features that influence listeners' physiology; fast-tempo music has a more consistent effect on cardiac and respiratory activity than slow-tempo music, and increased music intensity (loudness) tends to increase physiological arousal.

We also reviewed the relationship between listeners' emotional responses and physiological responses to music. Emotional response to music is an important motivator; listeners turn to music during exercise, during pain-invoking situations, and during mood induction. Physiological changes accompanying emotional responses to music tend to indicate a general change in arousal, rather than one tied to a specific emotion. For example, sudden increases in musical tempo or intensity may alter two listeners' heart rate similarly, while creating different emotional responses to the music. Music that elicits listeners' emotional response tends to do so via changes in tempo and intensity that correspond to changes in physiological arousal. One theoretical approach to music-induced emotional response holds that psychological processes such as the brainstem reflex, emotional contagion, episodic memory, and expectation violation mediate the emotional response to structural and acoustic features of music. Some studies suggest that the social environment of music listening affects physiological and emotional responses to music. Importantly, psychological mediation and social facilitation theory are not mutually exclusive in explaining how music impacts physiology and elicits emotional responses.

Activities such as music listening, music performance, and physical exercise can create a coupling between perception and action. Cardiac rhythms and respiration rates tend to be coupled and there is some evidence for their entrainment with the rates of body movement and musical sound. Sometimes entrainment between the motor and physiological systems and temporal features of the music results in decreased energy consumption during tasks such as dance or cycling. This may explain the increased performance in physical activities when people listen to music, especially with fast tempi. Other theoretical approaches postulate that music plays a motivational role in ways that affect energy expenditure.

Music also affects physiological markers of pain and stress. Listening to slow-tempo music can reduce physiological markers of stress following maximal exertion and can reduce pain and physiological markers of stress following medical procedures, faster than other musical tempi. However, subjective ratings of perceived pain often show more evidence of pain reduction during music listening than do physiological markers. Musical preference and familiarity are likely to be important factors to consider in future studies. Finally, neonatal infants in intensive care settings show reduced pain responses during medical procedures to music that contains slower tempo and simple rhythms; they also show accompanying reductions in physiological markers of stress that typically increase with pain.

Several music-physiology relationships have not yet been explored. Whether music can promote sleep and modulate physiology during sleep is a potential avenue for researchers who address sleep disorders. Time-of-day effects of music on physiology are also important to consider in future research, as individuals' baseline physiological activity shows daily (circadian) fluctuations; music may affect physiology differently depending upon the time of day as well as differentially impact the physiology of individuals whose circadian rhythms are out of phase with one another. A few studies have investigated how physiological responses to music are affected in group versus individual settings. More research as to how physiological responses to music may differ in group settings would yield a greater understanding of the social aspects of music listening. Researchers can also experimentally manipulate different musical features (such as tempo, intensity, musical genre) in passive as well as movement-based listening settings to better understand how music influences physiology. Individual differences in both music preferences and physiological activity suggest a need to titrate or adapt music applications at an individual level.

Finally, disorders of music perception provide tests of the role of physiology: specifically, whether the perceptual disorders are accompanied by physiological differences from normal perception. For example, some individuals exhibit beat deafness: an inability to move in time to a musical beat, despite normal hearing

(Phillips-Silver et al., 2011). These individuals show difficulty adapting to changes in musical tempo (Palmer et al., 2014) and exhibit altered event-related potential (ERP) responses to music (Mathias et al., 2016), although it is unknown whether other physiological responses are disrupted. Individuals with musical anhedonia, an inability to experience pleasure while listening to music, typically show a lack of physiological change in heart rate or skin conductance in response to chills-inducing music (Mas-Herrero et al., 2014). Although these disruptions to music perception are relatively rare (affecting less than 4 per cent of the population), these cases can be used to further test the theories reviewed here of physiological influences of music on perception and action.

Abbreviations

ANS	Autonomic Nervous System
BMRI-2	Brunel Music Rating Inventory
BP	Blood Pressure
BPM	Beats Per Minute (music)
dB SPL	Decibels of Sound Pressure Level
ECG	Electrocardiography
EDA	Electrodermal Activity
GSR	Galvanic Skin Response
HIIT	High-Intensity Interval Training
HR	Heart Rate
HRV	Heart Rate Variability
LRC	Locomotor-Respiratory Coupling
NICU	Neonatal Intensive Care Unit
NIPS	Neonate Infant Pain Scale
PIPP	Premature Infant Pain Profile
PNS	Parasympathetic Nervous System
RSA	Respiratory Sinus Arrythmia
SCL	Skin Conductance Level
SCR	Skin Conductance Rate
SDNN	Standard Deviation of Normal-to-Normal Intervals
SNS	Sympathetic Nervous System
STAI	State-Trait Anxiety Inventory

References

Almeida, F. A., Nunes, R. F., Ferreira, S., Krinski, K., Elsangedy, H. M., Buzzachera, C. F., Alves, R. C., & da Silva, S. G. (2015). Effects of musical tempo on physiological, affective, and perceptual variables and performance of self-selected walking pace. *Journal of Physical Therapy Science*, *27*(6), 1709–1712. http://doi.org/10.1589/jpts.27.1709

Amini, E., Rafiei, P., Zarei, K., Gohari, M., & Hamidi, M. (2013). Effect of lullaby and classical music on physiologic stability of hospitalized preterm infants: A randomized trial. *Journal of Neonatal-Perinatal Medicine*, *6*(4), 295–301. http://doi.org/10.3233/NPM-1371313

Arazi, H., Asadi, A., & Purabed, M. (2015). Physiological and psychophysical responses to listening to music during warm-up and circuit-type resistance exercise in strength trained men. *Journal of Sports Medicine*, *2015*, Article 389831. http://doi.org/10.1155/2015/389831

Bacon, C. J., Myers, T. R., & Karageorghis, I. (2012). Effect of music-movement synchrony on exercise oxygen consumption. *Journal of Sports Medicine and Physical Fitness*, *52*(4), 359–365.

Bannister, S. (2020). A vigilance explanation of musical chills? Effects of loudness and brightness manipulations. *Music and Science*, *3*, 1–17.

Bannister, S., & Eerola, T. (2018). Suppressing the chills: Effects of musical manipulation on the chills response. *Frontiers in Psychology*, *9*, 1–16 . http://doi.org/10.3389/fpsyg.2018.02046

Bardy, B. G., Hoffmann, C. P., Moens, B., Leman, M., & Dalla Bella, S. (2015). Sound-induced stabilization of breathing and moving. *Annals of the New York Academy of Sciences*, *1337*, 94–100. http://doi.org/10.1111/nyas.12650

Baumgartner, R., Reed, D. K., Tóth, B., Best, V., Majdak, P., Colburn, H. S., & Shinn-Cunningham, B. (2017). Asymmetries in behavioral and neural responses to spectral cues demonstrate the generality of auditory looming bias. *Proceedings of the National Academy of Sciences*, *114*(36), 9743–9748.

Beier, E. J., Janata, P., Hulbert, J. C., & Ferreira, F. (2020). Do you chill when I chill? A cross-cultural study of strong emotional responses to music. *Psychology of Aesthetics, Creativity, and the Arts*, 1–23 Advance online publication. http://doi.org/10.1037/aca0000310

Belfi, A. M., & Loui, P. (2020). Musical anhedonia and rewards of music listening: Current advances and a proposed model. *Annals of the New York Academy of Sciences*, *1464*, 99–114. http://doi.org/10.1111/nyas.14241

Bernardi, L., Porta, C., & Sleight, P. (2006). Cardiovascular, cerebrovascular, and respiratory changes induced by different types of music in musicians and non-musicians: The importance of silence. *Heart, 92*(4), 445–452. http://doi.org/10.1136/hrt.2005.064600

Bernardi, N. F., Bellemare-Pepin, A., & Peretz, I. (2017a). Enhancement of pleasure during spontaneous dance. *Frontiers in Human Neuroscience, 11*, 572. http://doi.org/10.3389/fnhum.2017.00572

Bernardi, N. F., Snow, S., Peretz, I., Orozco Perez, H. D., Sabet-Kassouf, N., & Lehmann, A. (2017b). Cardiorespiratory optimization during improvised singing and toning. *Scientific Reports, 7*(1), 8113. http://doi.org/10.1038/s41598-017-07171-2

Berntson, G. G., Thomas Bigger Jr, J., Eckberg, D. L., Grossman, P., Kaufmann, P. G., Malik, M. Malik, M., Nagaraja, H. N, Porges, S. W., Saul, J. P., Stone, P. H., & Van der Molen, M. W. 1. (1997). Heart rate variability: Origins, methods, and interpretive caveats. *Psychophysiology, 34*(6), 623–648. http://doi.org/10.1111/j.1469-8986.1997.tb02140.x

Bittman, E. L. (2021). Entrainment is NOT synchronization: An important distinction and its implications. *Journal of Biological Rhythms, 36*, 196–199.

Blasco-Lafarga, C., Garcia-Soriano, C., & Monteagudo, P. (2020). Autonomic modulation improves in response to harder performances while playing wind instruments. *Archives of Neuroscience, 7*(2), Article e101969. http://doi.org/10.5812/ans.101969

Blood, A. J., & Zatorre, R. J. (2001). Intensely pleasurable responses to music correlate with activity in brain regions implicated in reward and emotion. *Proceedings of the National Academy of Sciences of the United States of America, 98*(20), 11818–11823. http://doi.org/10.1073/pnas.191355898

Bood, R. J., Nijssen, M., van der Kamp, J., & Roerdink, M. (2013). The power of auditory-motor synchronization in sports: Enhancing running performance by coupling cadence with the right beats. *PloS One, 8*(8), Article e70758. http://doi.org/10.1371/journal.pone.0070758

Bradshaw, D. H., Donaldson, G. W., Jacobson, R. C., Nakamura, Y., & Chapman, C. R. (2011). Individual differences in the effects of music engagement on responses to painful stimulation. *Journal of Pain, 12*(12), 1262–1273. http://doi.org/10.1016/j.jpain.2011.08.010

Bradt, J., Dileo, C., Magill, L., & Teague, A. (2016). Music interventions for improving psychological and physical outcomes in cancer patients. *The Cochrane Database of Systematic Reviews, 8*, Article CD006911. http://doi.org/10.1002/14651858.CD006911.pub3

Bretherton, B., Deuchars, J., & Windsor, W. L. (2019). The effects of controlled tempo manipulations on cardiovascular autonomic function. *Music and Science*, *2*(1), 1–14. http://doi.org/10.1177/2059204319858281

Brupbacher, G., Harder, J., Faude, O., Zahner, L., & Donath, L. (2014). Music in CrossFit – Influence on performance, physiological, and psychological parameters. *Sports*, *2*(1), 14–23. http://doi.org/10.3390/sports2010014

Bullack, A., Büdenbender, N., Roden, I., & Kreutz, G. (2018). Psychophysiological responses to 'happy' and 'sad' music: A replication study. *Music Perception*, *35*(4), 502–517. http://doi.org/10.1525/mp.2018.35.4.502

Caumo, W., Schmidt, A. P., Schneider, C. N., Bergmann, J., Iwamoto, C. W., Adamatti, L. C., Bandeira, D., & Ferreira, M. B. (2001). Risk factors for postoperative anxiety in adults. *Anaesthesia*, *56*(8), 720–728. http://doi.org/10.1046/j.1365-2044.2001.01842.x

Cavaiuolo, C., Casani, A., Manso, G. D., & Orfeo, L. (2015). Effect of Mozart music on heel prick pain in preterm infants: A pilot randomized controlled trial. *Journal of Pediatric and Neonatal Individualized Medicine*, *4*(1), Article e040109. http://doi.org/10.7363/040109

Cervellin, G., & Lippi, G. (2011). From music-beat to heart-beat: A journey in the complex interactions between music, brain and heart. *European Journal of Internal Medicine*, *22*(4), 371–374. http://doi.org/10.1016/j.ejim.2011.02.019

Champagne, F. A., & Curley, J. P. (2009). Epigenetic mechanisms mediating the long-term effects of maternal care on development. *Neuroscience and Biobehavioral Reviews*, *33*(4), 593–600. http://doi.org/10.1016/j.neubiorev.2007.10.009

Cheng, T. H., & Tsai, C. G. (2016). Female listeners' autonomic responses to dramatic shifts between loud and soft music/sound passages: A study of heavy metal songs. *Frontiers in Psychology*, *7*, 182. http://doi.org/10.3389/fpsyg.2016.00182

Chtourou, H., Chaouachi, A., Hammouda, O., Chamari, K., & Souissi, N. (2012). Listening to music affects diurnal variation in muscle power output. *International Journal of Sports Medicine*, *33*(1), 43–47. http://doi.org/10.1055/s-0031-1284398

Chuen, L., Sears, D., & McAdams, S. (2016). Psychophysiological responses to auditory change. *Psychophysiology*, *53*(6), 891–904. http://doi.org/10.1111/psyp.12633

Coutinho, E., & Cangelosi, A. (2011). Musical emotions: Predicting second-by-second subjective feelings of emotion from low-level psychoacoustic features and physiological measurements. *Emotion*, *11*(4), 921–937. http://doi.org/10.1037/a0024700

Cowen, R., Stasiowska, M. K., Laycock, H., & Bantel, C. (2015). Assessing pain objectively: The use of physiological markers. *Anaesthesia, 70*(7), 828–847. http://doi.org/10.1111/anae.13018

Critchley, H., & Nagai, Y. (2013). Electrodermal activity (EDA). *Encyclopedia of Behavioral Medicine, 78,* 666–669. http://doi.org/10.1007/978-1-4419-1005-9

Cutrufello, P. T., Benson, B. A., & Landram, M. J. (2020). The effect of music on anaerobic exercise performance and muscular endurance. *Journal of Sports Medicine and Physical Fitness, 60*(3), 486–492. http://doi.org/10.23736/S0022-4707.19.10228-9

da Silva, A. G., Guida, H. L., Antônio, A. M., Marcomini, R. S., Fontes, A. M., de Abreu, L. C. Roque, A. K., Silva, S. B., Raimundo, R. D., Ferreira, C., & Valenti, V. E. (2014a). An exploration of heart rate response to differing music rhythm and tempos. *Complementary Therapies in Clinical Practice, 20*(2), 130–134. http://doi.org/10.1016/j.ctcp.2013.09.004

da Silva, S. A., Guida, H. L., Dos Santos Antonio, A. M., de Abreu, L. C., Monteiro, C. B., Ferreira, C. Ribeiro, V. F., Barnabe, V., Silva, S. B., Foncesca, F. L., Adami, F., Petenusso, M., Raimundo, R. D., & Valenti, V. E. (2014b). Acute auditory stimulation with different styles of music influences cardiac autonomic regulation in men. *International Cardiovascular Research Journal, 8*(3), 105–110.

Damm, L., Varoqui, D., De Cock, V. C., Dalla Bella, S., & Bardy, B. (2020). Why do we move to the beat? A multi-scale approach, from physical principles to brain dynamics. *Neuroscience and Biobehavioral Reviews, 112,* 553–584. http://doi.org/10.1016/j.neubiorev.2019.12.024

de Manzano, O., Theorell, T., Harmat, L., & Ullen, F. (2010). The psychophysiology of flow during piano playing. *Emotion, 10*(3), 301–311. http://doi.org/10.1037/a0018432

Dellacherie, D., Roy, M., Hugueville, L., Peretz, I., & Samson, S. (2011). The effect of musical experience on emotional self-reports and psychophysiological responses to dissonance. *Psychophysiology, 48*(3), 337–349. http://doi.org/10.1111/j.1469-8986.2010.01075.x

Desai, R., Thaker, R., Patel, J., & Parmar, J. (2015). Effect of music on post-exercise recovery rate in young healthy individuals. *International Journal of Research in Medical Sciences, 3*(4), 896–898. http://doi.org/10.5455/2320-6012.ijrms20150414

Di Cagno, A., Iuliano, E., Fiorilli, G., Aquino, G., Giombini, A., Menotti, F., Tsopani, D., & Calcagno, G. (2016). Effects of rhythmical and extra-rhythmical qualities of music on heart rate during stationary bike activities. *Journal of Sports Medicine and Physical Fitness, 56*(10), 1227–1231.

do Amaral, J. A., Guida, H. L., Vanderlei, F. M., Garner, D. M., de Abreu, L. C., & Valenti, V. E. (2015). The effects of musical auditory stimulation of different intensities on geometric indices of heart rate variability. *Alternative Therapies in Health and Medicine, 21*(5), 16–23.

Dyer, B. J., & McKune, A. J. (2013). Effects of music tempo on performance, psychological, and physiological variables during 20 km cycling in well-trained cyclists. *Perceptual and Motor Skills: Motor Skills & Ergonomics, 17*(2), 484–497. http://doi.org/10.2466/29.22.PMS.117x24z8

Ebert, D., Hefter, H., Binkofski, F., & Freund, H. J. (2002). Coordination between breathing and mental grouping of pianistic finger movements. *Perceptual and Motor Skills, 95*(2), 339–353. http://doi.org/10.2466/pms .2002.95.2.339

Eerola, T., & Vuoskoski, J. K. (2013). A review of music and emotion studies: Approaches, emotion models, and stimuli. *Music Perception, 30*(3), 307–340. http://doi.org/10.1525/mp.2012.30.3.307

Eerola, T., Vuoskoski, J. K., Peltola, H. R., Putkinen, V., & Schäfer, K. (2018). An integrative review of the enjoyment of sadness associated with music. *Physics of Life Reviews, 25*, 100–121. http://doi.org/10.1016/j.plrev.2017 .11.016

Egermann, H., Fernando, N., Chuen, L., & McAdams, S. (2015). Music induces universal emotion-related psychophysiological responses: Comparing Canadian listeners to Congolese Pygmies. *Frontiers in Psychology, 5*, 1341. http://doi.org/10.3389/fpsyg.2014.01341

Egermann, H., Pearce, M. T., Wiggins, G. A., & McAdams, S. (2013). Probabilistic models of expectation violation predict psychophysiological emotional responses to live concert music. *Cognitive, Affective and Behavioral Neuroscience, 13*(3), 533–553. http://doi.org/10.3758/s13415-013-0161-y

Egermann, H., Sutherland, M. E., Grewe, O., Nagel, F., Kopiez, R., & Altenmüller, E. (2011). Does music listening in a social context alter experience? A physiological and psychological perspective on emotion. *Musicae Scientiae, 15*(3), 307–323. http://doi.org/10.1177/1029864911 399497

Eliakim, M., Bodner, E., Eliakim, A., Nemet, D., & Meckel, Y. (2012). Effect of motivational music on lactate levels during recovery from intense exercise. *Journal of Strength and Conditioning Research, 26*(1), 80–86. http://doi.org /10.1519/JSC.0b013e31821d5f31

Eliakim, M., Bodner, E., Meckel, Y., Nemet, D., & Eliakim, A. (2013). Effect of rhythm on the recovery from intense exercise. *Journal of Strength and Conditioning Research, 27*(4), 1019–1024. http://doi.org/10.1519/JSC .0b013e318260b829

Friberg, A., & Sundberg, J. (1999). Does music performance allude to locomotion? A model of final ritardandi derived from measurements of stopping runners. *Journal of the Acoustical Society of America*, *105*, 1469–1484. http://doi.org/10.1121/1.426687

Fritz, T. H., Hardikar, S., Demoucron, M., Niessen, M., Demey, M., Giot, Ol., Li, Y., Haynes, J.-D., Villringer, A., & Leman, M. (2013). Musical agency reduces perceived exertion during strenuous physical performance. *Proceedings of the National Academy of Sciences of the United States of America*, *110*(44), 17784–17789. http://doi.org/10.1073/pnas.1217252110

Garcia, R. L., & Hand, C. J. (2016). Anagelsic effects of self-chosen music type on cold pressor-induced pain: Motivating vs. relaxing music. *Psychology of Music*, *44*(5), 967–983. http://doi.org/10.1177/0305735615602144

Garza-Villarreal, E. A., Pando, V., Vuust, P., & Parsons, C. (2017). Music-induced analgesia in chronic pain conditions: A systematic review and meta-analysis. *Pain Physician*, *20*(7), 597–610.

Gąsior, J. S., Sacha, J., Jeleń, P. J., Zieliński, J., & Przybylski, J. (2016). Heart rate and respiratory rate influence on heart rate variability repeatability: Effects of the correction for the prevailing heart rate. *Frontiers in Physiology*, *7*, 356. http://doi.org/10.3389/fphys.2016.00356

Goodwin, M. L., Harris, J. E., Hernández, A., & Gladden, L. B. (2007). Blood lactate measurements and analysis during exercise: A guide for clinicians. *Journal of Diabetes Science and Technology*, *1*(4), 558–569. http://doi.org/10.1177/193229680700100414

Guhn, M., Hamm, A., & Zentner, M. (2007). Physiological and musico-acoustic correlates of the chill response. *Music Perception*, *24*(5), 473–483. http://doi.org/10.1525/mp.2007.24.5.473

Harmat, L., Ullén, F., de Manzano, Ö., Olsson, E. von Schéele, B., & Theorell, T. (2011). Heart rate variability during piano playing: A case study of three professional solo pianists playing a self-selected and a difficult prima vista piece. *Music and Medicine*, *3*(2), 102–107. http://doi.org/10.1177/1943862110387158

Hartling, L., Shaik, M. S., Tjosvold, L., Leicht, R., Liang, Y., & Kumar, M. (2009). Music for medical indications in the neonatal period: A systematic review of randomised controlled trials. *Archives of Disease in Childhood, Fetal and Neonatal Edition*, *94*(5), F349–F354. http://doi.org/10.1136/adc.2008.148411

Hoffmann, C. P., & Bardy, B. G. (2015). Dynamics of the locomotor–respiratory coupling at different frequencies. *Experimental Brain Research*, *233*(5), 1551–1561. http://doi.org/10.1007/s00221-015-4229-5

Hoffmann, C. P., Torregrosa, G., & Bardy, B. G. (2012). Sound stabilizes locomotor-respiratory coupling and reduces energy cost. *PloS One, 7*(9), Article e45206. http://doi.org/10.1371/journal.pone.0045206

Hutchinson, J. C., & O'Neil, B. J. (2020). Effects of respite music during recovery between bouts of intense exercise. *Sport, Exercise, and Performance Psychology, 9*(1), 102–114. http://doi.org/10.1037/spy00 00161

Jacobs, I. (1986). Blood lactate. *Sports Medicine, 3*(1), 10–25.

Jones, L., Tiller, N. B., & Karageorghis, C. I. (2017). Psychophysiological effects of music on acute recovery from high-intensity interval training. *Physiology and Behavior, 170,* 106–114. http://doi.org/10.1016/j.physbeh .2016.12.017

Juslin, P. N. (2013). From everyday emotions to aesthetic emotions: Towards a unified theory of musical emotions. *Physics of Life Reviews, 10*(3), 235–266. http://doi.org/10.1016/j.plrev.2013.05.008

Juslin, P. N., Barradas, G., & Eerola, T. (2015). From sound to significance: Exploring the mechanisms underlying emotional reactions to music. *The American Journal of Psychology, 128*(3), 281–304. http://doi.org/10.5406 /amerjpsyc.128.3.0281

Juslin, P. N., Harmat, L., & Eerola, T. (2014). What makes music emotionally significant? Exploring the underlying mechanisms. *Psychology of Music, 42* (4), 599–623. http://doi.org/10.1177/0305735613484548

Karageorghis, C. I., Bruce, A. C., Pottratz, S. T., Stevens, R. C., Bigliassi, M., & Hamer, M. (2018). Psychological and psychophysiological effects of recuperative music postexercise. *Medicine and Science in Sports and Exercise, 50* (4), 739–746. http://doi.org/10.1249/MSS.0000000000001497

Karageorghis, C. I., Jones, L., Priest, D. L., Akers, R. I., Clarke, A., Perry, J. M., Reddick, B. T., Bishop, D. T., & Lim, H. B. (2011). Revisiting the relationship between exercise heart rate and music tempo preference. *Research Quarterly for Exercise and Sport, 82*(2), 274–284. http://doi.org/10.1080 /02701367.2011.10599755

Karageorghis, C. I., & Priest, D. L. (2012a). Music in the exercise domain: A review and synthesis (Part I). *International Review of Sport and Exercise Psychology, 5*(1), 44–66. http://doi.org/10.1080/1750984X .2011.631026

Karageorghis, C. I., & Priest, D. L. (2012b). Music in the exercise domain: A review and synthesis (Part II). *International Review of Sport and Exercise Psychology, 5*(1), 67–84. http://doi.org/10.1080/1750984X .2011.631027

Koelsch, S., & Jäncke, L. (2015). Music and the heart. *European Heart Journal*, *36*(44), 3043–3049. http://doi.org/10.1093/eurheartj/ehv430

Krabs, R. U., Enk, R., Teich, N., & Koelsch, S. (2015). Autonomic effects of music in health and Crohn's disease: The impact of isochronicity, emotional valence, and tempo. *PloS One*, *10*(5), Article e0126224. http://doi.org/10.1371/journal.pone.0126224

Lã, F. M., & Gill, B. (2019). Physiology and its impact on the performance of singing. In G. F. Welch, D. M. Howard, & J. Nix (Eds.), *Oxford handbooks online: The Oxford handbook of singing* (pp. 1–20). Oxford University Press. http://doi.org/10.1093/oxfordhb/9780199660773.013.23

Labbé, C., Trost, W., & Grandjean, D. (2020). Affective experiences to chords are modulated by mode, meter, tempo, and subjective entrainment. *Psychology of Music*, *49*(4):1–16. http://doi.org/10.1177/0305735620906887

Labrague, L. J., & McEnroe-Petitte, D. M. (2016). Influence of music on preoperative anxiety and physiologic parameters in women undergoing gynecologic surgery. *Clinical Nursing Research*, *25*(2), 157–173. http://doi.org/10.1177/1054773814544168

Landis-Shack, N., Heinz, A. J., & Bonn-Miller, M. O. (2017). Music therapy for posttraumatic stress in adults: A theoretical review. *Psychomusicology: Music, Mind, and Brain*, *27*(4), 334.

Lang, P. J., Bradley, M. M., & Cuthbert, B. N. (1997). International affective picture system (IAPS): Technical manual and affective ratings. *Center for Research in Psychophysiology.*

Lee, S., & Kimmerly, D. S. (2016). Influence of music on maximal self-paced running performance and passive post-exercise recovery rate. *Journal of Sports Medicine and Physical Fitness*, *56*(1–2), 39–48.

Lee, W. P., Wu, P. Y., Lee, M. Y., Ho, L. H., & Shih, W. M. (2017). Music listening alleviates anxiety and physiological responses in patients receiving spinal anesthesia. *Complementary Therapies in Medicine*, *31*, 8–13. http://doi.org/10.1016/j.ctim.2016.12.006

Leow, L. A., Waclawik, K., & Grahn, J. A. (2018). The role of attention and intention in synchronization to music: Effects on gait. *Experimental Brain Research*, *236*(1), 99–115. http://doi.org/10.1007/s00221-017-5110-5

Lim, H. B., Karageorghis, C. I., Romer, L. M., & Bishop, D. T. (2014). Psychophysiological effects of synchronous versus asynchronous music during cycling. *Medicine and Science in Sports and Exercise*, *46*(2), 407–413. http://doi.org/10.1016/j.ctim.2016.12.006

Lima, L. S., Correia, V. O., Nascimento, T. K., Chaves, B., Silva, J. R., Alves, J. A., Dantas, D., & Ribeiro, M. D. (2017). Is music effective for pain relief in burn victims? *International Archives of Medicine*, *10*(11), 1–10. http://doi.org/10.3823/2281

Lundqvist, L.-O., Carlsson, F., Hilmersson, P., & Juslin, P. N. (2009). Emotional responses to music: Experience, expression, and physiology. *Psychology of Music*, *37*(1), 61–90. http://doi.org/10.1177/0305735607086048

Lynar, E., Cvejic, E., Schubert, E., & Vollmer-Conna, U. (2017). The joy of heartfelt music: An examination of emotional and physiological responses. *International Journal of Psychophysiology*, *120*, 118–125. http://doi.org/10.1016/j.ijpsycho.2017.07.012

Martiniano, E. C., Santana, M. D. R., Barros, É. L. D., da Silva, M. D. S., Garner, D. M., De Abreu, L. C., & Valenti, V. E. (2018). Musical auditory stimulus acutely influences heart rate dynamic responses to medication in subjects with well-controlled hypertension. *Scientific Reports*, *8*(1), 1–9.

Mas-Herrero, E., Zatorre, R. J., Rodriguez-Fornells, A., & Marco-Pallarés, J. (2014). Dissociation between musical and monetary reward responses in specific musical anhedonia. *Current Biology*, *24*, 699–704.

Mathias, B., Lidji, P., Honing, H., Palmer, C., & Peretz, I. (2016). Electrical brain responses to beat irregularities in two cases of beat deafness. *Frontiers in Neuroscience*, *10*, 40. http://doi.org/10.3389/fnins.2016.00040

Mendoza, A., Santoyo, F. L., Agulló, A., Fenández-Cañamaque, J. L., & Vivó, C. (2016). The management of pain associated with wound care in severe burn patients in Spain. *International Journal of Burns and Trauma*, *6* (1), 1–10.

Mikutta, C. A., Schwab, S., Niederhauser, S., Wuermle, O., Strik, W., & Altorfer, A. (2013). Music, perceived arousal, and intensity: Psychophysiological reactions to Chopin's 'Tristesse'. *Psychophysiology*, *50*(9), 909–919. http://doi.org/10.1111/psyp.12071

Mitchell, M. (2003). Patient anxiety and modern elective surgery: A literature review. *Journal of Clinical Nursing*, *12*(6), 806–815. http://doi.org/10.1046/j.1365-2702.2003.00812.x

Moens, B., Muller, C., van Noorden, L., Franĕk, M., Celie, B., Boone, J. Bourgois, J., & Leman, M. (2014). Encouraging spontaneous synchronisation with D-Jogger, an adaptive music player that aligns movement and music. *PloS One*, *9*(12), Article e114234. http://doi.org/10.1371/journal.pone.0114234

Mollakazemi, M. J., Biswal, D., Elayi, S. C., Thyagarajan, S., & Evans, J. (2019). Synchronization of autonomic and cerebral rhythms during listening to music: Effects of tempo and cognition of songs. *Physiological Research*, *68*(6), 1005–1019. http://doi.org/10.33549/physiolres.934163

Müller, V., & Lindenberger, U. (2011). Cardiac and respiratory patterns synchronize between persons during choir singing. *PloS One, 6*(9), Article e24893. http://doi.org/10.1371/journal.pone.0024893

Mütze, H., Kopiez, R., & Wolf, A. (2018). The effect of a rhythmic pulse on the heart rate: Little evidence for rhythmical 'entrainment' and 'synchronization'. *Musicae Scientiae, 24*(3), 377–400. http://doi.org/10.1177/10298649 18817805

Nakahara, H., Furuya, S., Masuko, T., Francis, P. R., & Kinoshita, H. (2011). Performing music can induce greater modulation of emotion-related psychophysiological responses than listening to music. *International Journal of Psychophysiology, 81*, 152–158. http://doi.org/10.1016/j.ijpsycho.2011.06 .003

Nassrallah, F., Comeau, G., Russell, D., & Cossette, I. (2013). Coordination of breathing and various movement markers during pianists' performance tasks. *Perceptual and Motor Skills, 116*(1), 1–20. http://doi.org/10.2466/22 .25.26.PMS.116.1.1-20

Nilsson, U. (2008). The anxiety- and pain-reducing effects of music interventions: A systematic review. *AORN Journal, 87*(4), 780–807. http://doi.org/10 .1016/j.aorn.2007.09.013

Nomura, S., Yoshimura, K., & Kurosawa, Y. (2013). A pilot study on the effect of music-heart beat feedback system on human heart activity. *Journal of Medical Informatics and Technologies, 22*, 251–256.

Olsen, K. N., & Stevens, C. J. (2013). Psychophysiological response to acoustic intensity change in a musical chord. *Journal of Psychophysiology, 27*(1), 16–26. http://doi.org/10.1027/0269-8803/a000082

Olson, R. L., Brush, C. J., O'Sullivan, D. J., & Alderman, B. L. (2015). Psychophysiological and ergogenic effects of music in swimming. *Comparative Exercise Physiology, 11*(2), 79–87. http://doi.org/10.3920 /CEP150003

Omigie, D. (2016). Basic, specific, mechanistic? Conceptualizing musical emotions in the brain. *Journal of Comparative Neurology, 524*(8), 1676–1686. http://doi.org/10.1002/cne.23854

O'Toole, A., Francis, K., & Pugsley, L. (2017). Does music positively impact preterm infant outcomes? *Advances in Neonatal Care, 17*(3), 192–202. http:// doi.org/10.1097/ANC.0000000000000394

Ooishi, Y., Mukai, H., Watanabe, K., Kawato, S., & Kashino, M. (2017). Increase in salivary oxytocin and decrease in salivary cortisol after listening to relaxing slow-tempo and exciting fast-tempo music. *PloS One, 12*(12), Article e0189075. http://doi.org/10.1371/journal.pone.0189075

Palmer, C., Lidji, P., & Peretz, I. (2014). Losing the beat: Deficits in temporal coordination. *Philosophical Transactions of the Royal Society B, 369*, 1658. http://doi.org/10.1098/rstb.2013.0405

Panskepp, J. (1995). The emotional sources of 'chills' induced by music. *Music Perception, 13*(2), 171–207. http://doi.org/10.2307/40285693

Patania, V. M., Padulo, J., Iuliano, E., Ardigò, L. P., Čular, D., Miletić, A., & De Giorgio, A. (2020). The psychophysiological effects of different tempo music on endurance versus high-intensity performances. *Frontiers in Psychology, 11*, 74, 1–7. http://doi.org/10.3389/fpsyg.2020.00074

Phillips-Silver, J., Toiviainen, P., Gosselin, N., Piché, O., Nozaradan, S., Palmer, C., & Peretz, I. (2011). Born to dance but beat deaf: A new form of congenital amusia. *Neuropsychologia, 49*, 961–969. http://doi.org/10.1016/j.neuropsychologia.2011.02.002

Pölkki, T., & Korhonen, A. (2012). The effectiveness of music on pain among preterm infants in the neonatal intensive care unit: A systematic review. *JBI Library of Systematic Reviews, 10*(58), 4600–4609. http://doi.org/10.11124/jbisrir-2012-428

Porges, S. W. (2007). The polyvagal perspective. *Biological Psychology, 74*(2), 116–143. http://doi.org/10.1016/j.biopsycho.2006.06.009

Rasteiro, F. M., Messias, L. H., Scariot, P. P., Cruz, J. P., Cetein, R. L., Gobatto, C. A., & Manchado-Gobatto, F. B. (2020). Effects of preferred music on physiological responses, perceived exertion, and anaerobic threshold determination in an incremental running test on both sexes. *PloS One, 15* (8), Article e0237310. http://doi.org/10.1371/journal.pone.0237310

Rauscher, F. H., Shaw, G. L., & Ky, K. N. (1993). Music and spatial task performance. *Nature, 365*(6447), 611. http://doi.org/10.1038/365611a0

Rossi, A., Molinaro, A., Savi, E., Micheletti, S., Galli, J., Chirico, G., & Fazzi, E. (2018). Music reduces pain perception in healthy newborns: A comparison between different music tracks and recoded heartbeat. *Early Human Development, 124*, 7–10. http://doi.org/10.1016/j.earlhumdev.2018.07.006

Roy, M., Peretz, I., & Rainville, P. (2008). Emotional valence contributes to music-induced analgesia. *Pain, 134*(1–2), 140–147. http://doi.org/10.1016/j.pain.2007.04.003

Ruiz-Blais, S., Orini, M., & Chew, E. (2020). Heart rate variability synchronizes when non-experts vocalize together. *Frontiers in Physiology, 11*, 1–12. http://doi.org/10.3389/fphys.2020.00762

Saarikallio, S. (2011). Music as emotional self-regulation throughout adulthood. *Psychology of Music, 39*(3), 307–327. http://doi.org/10.1177/0305735610374894

Sachs, M. E., Damasio, A., & Habibi, A. (2015). The pleasures of sad music: A systematic review. *Frontiers in Human Neuroscience, 9*, 404. http://doi.org/10.3389/fnhum.2015.00404

Salimpoor, V. N., Zald, D. H., Zatorre, R. J., Dagher, A., & McIntosh, A. R. (2015). Predictions and the brain: How musical sounds become rewarding. *Trends in Cognitive Sciences, 19*(2), 86–91. http://doi.org/10.1016/j.tics.2014.12.001

Samuels, E. R., Hou, R. H., Langley, R. W., Szabadi, E., & Bradshaw, C. M. (2007). Modulation of the acoustic startle response by the level of arousal: Comparison of clonidine and modafinil in healthy volunteers. *Neuropsychopharmacology, 32*(11), 2405–2421. http://doi.org/10.1038/sj.npp.1301363

Santana, M. D., Martiniano, E. C., Monteiro, L. R., Valenti, V. E., Garner, D. M., Sorpreso, I. C., & de Abreu, L. C. (2017). Musical auditory stimulation influences heart rate autonomic responses to endodontic treatment. *Evidence-Based Complementary and Alternative Medicine, 2017*, Article 4847869. http://doi.org/10.1155/2017/4847869

Savitha, D., Mallikarjuna, R. N., & Rao, C. (2010). Effect of different musical tempo on post-exercise recovery in young adults. *Indian Journal of Physiology and Pharmacology, 54*(1), 32–36.

Savitha, D., Sejil, T. V., Rao, S., Roshan, C. J., & Avadhany, S. T. (2013). The effect of vocal and instrumental music on cardio respiratory variables, energy expenditure and exertion levels during sub maximal treadmill exercise. *Indian Journal of Physiology and Pharmacology, 57*(2), 159–168.

Scheurich, R., Zamm, A., & Palmer, C. (2018). Tapping into rate flexibility: Musical training facilitates synchronization around spontaneous production rates. *Frontiers in Psychology, 9*(458), 1–13.

Shabani, F., Nayeri, N. D., Karimi, R., Zarei, K., & Chehrazi, M. (2016). Effects of music therapy on pain responses induced by blood sampling in premature infants: A randomized cross-over trial. *Iranian Journal of Nursing and Midwifery Research, 21*(4), 391–396. http://doi.org/10.4103/1735-9066.185581

Shaffer, F., McCraty, R., & Zerr, C. L. (2014). A healthy heart is not a metronome: An integrative review of the heart's anatomy and heart rate variability. *Frontiers in Psychology, 5*, 1040. http://doi.org/10.3389/fpsyg.2014.01040

Shove, P., & Repp, B. (1995). Musical motion and performance: Theoretical and empirical perspectives. In J. Rink (Ed.), *The practice of performance: Studies in musical interpretation* (pp. 55–83). Cambridge University Press. http://doi.org/10.1017/CBO9780511552366.004

Sills, D., & Todd, A. (2015). Does music directly affect a person's heart rate? *Journal of Emerging Investigators*, 1–4. www.emerginginvestigators.org/art icles/does-music-directly-affect-a-person-s-heart-rate

Solberg, R., & Dibben, N. (2019). Peak experiences with electronic dance music: Subjective experiences, physiological responses, and musical characteristics of the break routine. *Music Perception*, *36*(4), 371–389. http://doi .org/10.1525/mp.2019.36.4.371

Stork, M. J., Karageorghis, C. I., & Martin Ginis, K. A. (2019). Let's go: Psychological, psychophysical, and physiological effects of music during sprint interval exercise. *Psychology of Sport and Exercise*, *45*, Article 101547. http://doi.org/10.1016/j.psychsport.2019.101547

Swaminathan, S., & Schellenberg, E. G. (2015). Current emotion research in music psychology. *Emotion Review*, *7*(2), 189–197. http://doi.org/10.1177 /1754073914558282

Tan, F., Tengah, A., Nee, L. Y., & Fredericks, S. (2014). A study of the effect of relaxing music on heart rate recovery after exercise among healthy students. *Complementary Therapies in Clinical Practice*, *20*(2), 114–117. http://doi .org/10.1016/j.ctcp.2014.01.001

Tang, L., Wang, H., Liu, Q., Wang, F., Wang, M., Sun, J., & Zhao, L. (2018). Effect of music intervention on pain responses in premature infants undergoing placement procedures of peripherally inserted central venous catheter: A randomized controlled trial. *European Journal of Integrative Medicine*, *19*, 105–109. http://doi.org/10.1016/j.eujim.2018 .03.006

Task Force of the European Society of Cardiology and the North American Society of Pacing and Electrophysiology. (1996). Heart rate variability: Standards of measurement, physiological interpretation, and clinical use. *Circulation*, *93*, 1043–1065.

Tekgündüz, K. Ş., Polat, S., Gürol, A., & Apay, S. E. (2019). Oral glucose and listening to lullaby to decrease pain in preterm infants supported with NCPAP: A randomized controlled trial. *Pain Management Nursing*, *20*(1), 54–61. http://doi.org/10.1016/j.pmn.2018.04.008

Terry, P. C., Karageorghis, C. I., Curran, M. L., Martin, O. V., & Parsons-Smith, R. L. (2020). Effects of music in exercise and sport: A meta-analytic review. *Psychological Bulletin*, *146*(2), 91–117. http://doi.org/10.1037/bul0000216

Terry, P. C., Karageorghis, C. I., Mecozzi Saha, A., & D'Auria, S. (2012). Effects of synchronous music on treadmill running among elite triathletes. *Journal of Science and Medicine in Sport*, *15*(1), 52–57. http://doi.org/10 .1016/j.jsams.2011.06.003

Thompson, W. F., Schellenberg, E. G., & Husain, G. (2001). Arousal, mood, and the Mozart effect. *Psychological Science, 12*(3), 248–251. http://doi.org /10.1111/1467-9280.00345

Trappe, H. J. (2010). The effects of music on the cardiovascular system and cardiovascular health. *Heart, 96*(23), 1868–1871. http://doi.org/10.1136/hrt .2010.209858

Trehub, S. E., Ghazban, N., & Corbeil, M. (2015). Musical affect regulation in infancy. *Annals of the New York Academy of Sciences, 1337*, 186–192. http:// doi.org/10.1111/nyas.12622

Trost, W., Labbé, C., & Grandjean, D. (2017). Rhythmic entrainment as a musical affect induction mechanism. *Neuropsychologia, 96*, 96–110. http://doi.org/10.1016/j.neuropsychologia.2017.01.004

Tsai, C.-G., & Chen, C.-P. (2015). Musical tension over time: Listeners' physiological responses to the 'retransition' in classical sonata form. *Journal of New Music Research, 44*(3), 271–276. http://doi.org/10.1080 /09298215.2015.1043310

Turpin, G., Schaefer, F., & Boucsein, W. (1999). Effects of stimulus intensity, risetime, and duration on autonomic and behavioral responding: Implications for the differentiation of orienting, startle, and defense responses. *Psychophysiology, 36*(4), 453–463.

Valenti, V. E., Guida, H. L., Frizzo, A. C., Cardoso, A. C., Vanderlei, L. C., & Abreu, L. C. (2012). Auditory stimulation and cardiac autonomic regulation. *Clinics, 67*(8), 955–958. http://doi.org/10.6061/clinics/2012(08)16

van der Zwaag, M. D., Westerink, J. H. D. M., & van den Broek, E. L. (2011). Emotional and psychophysiological responses to tempo, mode, and percussiveness. *Musicae Scientiae, 15*(2), 250–269. http://doi.org/10.1177 /1029864911403364

Van Dyck, E., & Leman, M. (2016). Ergogenic effect of music during running performance. *Annals of Sports Medicine and Research, 3*(6), 1082–1085.

Van Dyck, E., Six, J., Soyer, E., Denys, M., Bardijn, I., & Leman, M. (2017). Adopting a music-to-heart rate alignment strategy to measure the impact of music and its tempo on human heart rate. *Musicae Scientiae, 21*(4), 390–404. http://doi.org/10.1177/1029864917700706

Vickhoff, B., Malmgren, H., Aström, R. Nyberg, G., Ekström, Engwall, M., Snygg, J., Nilsson, M., & Jörnsten, R. (2013). Music structure determines heart rate variability of singers. *Frontiers in Psychology, 4*, 1–16. http://doi .org/10.3389/fpsyg.2013.00334

Vieillard, S., Roy, M., & Peretz, I. (2012). Expressiveness in musical emotions. *Psychological Research, 76*, 641–653. http://doi.org/10.1007/s00426-011-0361-4

Vuilleumier, P., & Trost, W. (2015). Music and emotions: From enchantment to entrainment. *Annals of the New York Academy of Sciences, 1337*, 212–222. http://doi.org/10.1111/nyas.12676

Wang, Y., Wei, J., Guan, X., Zhang, Y., Zhang, Y., Zhang, N. Mao, M., Du, W., Ren, Y., Shen, H., & Liu, P. (2020). Music intervention in pain relief of cardiovascular patients in cardiac procedures: A systematic review and meta-analysis. *Pain Medicine, 21*(11), 3055–3065. Advance online publication. http://doi.org/10.1093/pm/pnaa148

Watanabe, K., Ooishi, Y., & Kashino, M. (2015). Sympathetic tone induced by high acoustic tempo requires fast respiration. *PloS One, 10*(8), Article e0135589. http://doi.org/10.1371/journal.pone.0135589

Watanabe, K., Ooishi, Y., & Kashino, M. (2017). Heart rate responses induced by acoustic tempo and its interaction with basal heart rate. *Scientific Reports, 7*, Article 43856. http://doi.org/10.1038/srep43856

Waterhouse, J., Hudson, P., & Edwards, B. (2010). Effects of music tempo upon submaximal cycling performance. *Scandinavian Journal of Medicine and Science in Sports, 20*(4), 662–669. http://doi.org/10.1111/j.1600-0838 .2009.00948.x

Welch, G.F., Howard, D.M., & Nix, J. (Eds.), *Oxford handbooks online: The Oxford handbook of singing*. Oxford University Press. http://doi.org/10.1093 /oxfordhb/9780199660773.013.23

White, E. L., & Rickard, N. S. (2016). Emotion response and regulation to 'happy' and 'sad' music stimuli: Partial synchronization of subjective and physiological responses. *Musicae Scientiae, 20*(1), 11–25. http://doi.org/10 .1177/1029864915608911

Wolfe, J., Garnier, M., & Smith, J. (2009). Vocal tract resonances in speech, singing, and playing musical instruments. *HFSP, 3*(1): 6–23.

Wright, S. E., & Palmer, C. (2020). Physiological and behavioral factors in musicians' performance tempo. *Frontiers in Human Neuroscience, 14*, 1–15. http://doi.org/10.3389/fnhum.2020.00311

Wu, P. Y., Huang, M. L., Lee, W. P., Wang, C., & Shih, W. M. (2017). Effects of music listening on anxiety and physiological responses in patients undergoing awake craniotomy. *Complementary Therapies in Medicine, 32*, 56–60. http://doi.org/10.1016/j.ctim.2017.03.007

Zatorre, R. J. (2015). Musical pleasure and reward: Mechanisms and dysfunction. *Annals of the New York Academy of Sciences, 1337*, 202–211. http://doi.org/10.1111/nyas.12677

Zatorre, R. J., & Salimpoor, V. N. (2013). From perception to pleasure: Music and its neural substrates. *Proceedings of the National Academy of Sciences of* the United States of America, *110*(Suppl. 2), 10430–10437. http://doi.org/10.1073/pnas.1301228110

Zekveld, A. A., Koelewijn, T., & Kramer, S. E. (2018). The pupil dilation response to auditory stimuli: Current state of knowledge. *Trends in Hearing*, *22*, 1–25. http://doi.org/10.1177/2331216518777174

Acknowledgements

This work was supported by NSERC Grant 298173 and a Canada Research Chair award to C. Palmer and an NSERC-CREATE postdoctoral scholarship to V. Bégel. We thank Jocelyne Chan, Clara Freeman, and Lee Whitehorne for comments on an earlier draft.

Cambridge Elements ☰

Perception

James T. Enns
The University of British Columbia
Editor James T. Enns is Professor at the University of British Columbia, where he researches the interaction of perception, attention, emotion, and social factors. He has previously been Editor of the *Journal of Experimental Psychology: Human Perception and Performance* and an Associate Editor at *Psychological Science, Consciousness and Cognition, Attention Perception & Psychophysics,* and *Visual Cognition.*

Editorial Board

About the Series

The modern study of human perception includes event perception, bidirectional influences between perception and action, music, language, the integration of the senses, human action observation, and the important roles of emotion, motivation, and social factors. Each Element in the series combines authoritative literature reviews of foundational topics with forward-looking presentations of the recent developments on a given topic.

Cambridge Elements ≡

Perception

Elements in the Series

Printed in the United States
by Baker & Taylor Publisher Services